Confessions of a Recovered Youth Pastor

Confessions of a Recovered Youth Pastor

by Ferd Motley, as told to Steve McLachlan

iUniverse, Inc.
New York Lincoln Shanghai

Confessions of a Recovered Youth Pastor

All Rights Reserved © 2003 by Steve McLachlan

No part of this book may be reproduced or transmitted in any form or by any means, graphic, electronic, or mechanical, including photocopying, recording, taping, or by any information storage retrieval system, without the written permission of the publisher.

iUniverse, Inc.

For information address:
iUniverse, Inc.
2021 Pine Lake Road, Suite 100
Lincoln, NE 68512
www.iuniverse.com

ISBN: 0-595-29401-4

Printed in the United States of America

Contents

Foreword. vii
The Call 1
Youth Group Discipline 5
The Bus 9
Never Assume 14
Special Rules for Girls 18
The Youth Group Cookbook 22
The Don'ts of Mission Trip 27
Help!. 32
O Christmas Tree 37
The Hats You Wear 41
Heavy Metal Christians. 46
My Favorite Games 50
The Walkathon. 55
Tubing On The River 59
The Office. 64
Thieves!. 69
Bible Learning Activities 74
Preaching 78

Taking Care of Ferd 84
It's Not My Fault! 87
A Never-Ending Story 91

Foreword

"Hello, my name is Pastor Ferd, and it's been 12 years since I was a Youth Pastor."

This is a book of youth worker experiences—mainly mistakes—dedicated to everyone out there busy making their own mistakes in youth ministry. Those of you who have been there might really appreciate it. You'll find yourself in these stories, and maybe even wonder if you wrote some of them, then forgot. Partial amnesia is not uncommon after traumatic events. One theory says even the Apostle Paul was affected, and would have included "and some to be youth pastors…" in Ephesians 4:11, except he had not yet had time to recover from his own mental block.

I've been recovered long enough to realize I'm not alone. My therapist tells me there are several of us, most just don't like to come out of hiding. Relating these stories is supposed to help.

Those of you entering youth ministry might need to read this. In fact, at Youth Pastor U. this ought to be required reading! But I forget myself. Youth Pastor U. is Youth Pastor You, since you may be all the training you're going to get. The campus is the church that is so sure you will do a good job, and your professors are between the ages of 12 and 18.

Sometimes I'll see a Youth Pastor giving it all he's got: praying, preaching, teaching, playing, driving, song-leading, cooking, planning, and starving—and feeling like a total failure. My heart goes out to you. You need to know you're not alone, doing the Star Trek thing, "Where no man has gone before." We who have been there understand, we care, and when we see you, we pray for you. But we can't join you. It doesn't take much of a slip to fall off the wagon.

The stories in this book are all true, or at least they're true to my memory. Names have been changed to protect me from lawsuit, and occasionally things are slightly embellished, but at heart they are true. If anyone correctly identifies themselves in one of these stories, I'd love to hear from you! Some of you I've kept in touch with, some I don't have a clue. If you think you should get some money for being written about, write your own book! Otherwise, I will go so far as to give you a copy and buy you lunch.

The Call

"Let me be sure I've got this right: you'll give me $800 a month, you want 40 hours a week, you want me to go to Bible College but you won't pay for it, and I've got a wife and three kids to support. And you're calling this an offer? Let me get back to you."

First, you should understand that my vast credentials for youth work about equaled my credentials for nuclear physics or deep-sea exploration.

Raised Catholic, third of nine kids, I attended Catholic grade school for eight years, going to Mass every schoolday, and sometimes on Sunday. Like so many others, when I graduated Catholic school, I graduated church, too. I tried a Midnight Mass once, but didn't like it. In High School I tried Youth Group once to please a girlfriend, but something went wrong when I told a joke that my friends thought funny. And there was that dance at a Mormon church. That about sums up my experience with Youth Group before receiving this job offer, thinly disguised as a "Call."

I did have some church experience. As if I drew a card in a board game, I skipped Youth Group and went straight to Young Marrieds! I was still 18 when my fiancée Sweetie, a friend of hers, and a friend of a friend of hers dragged me to this College and Career Bible Study sponsored by the First Big Church on the Corner. I didn't want to go, and made them promise they'd never bug me about it again if I went this once. That night I took Jesus Christ as my Savior. Since then, it's been more a matter of Him taking me—on a roller-coaster ride!

Fast-forward six years, to the exciting world of Christian radio (Call letters: KASH)! It turns out radio is not always exciting. I took the job to be a D.J., but got only an hour and a half to play records (Records are black vinyl things we used in the old days to make music), make announcements, run contests and give stuff away. I liked that part of the job. Unfortunately programs paid the bills while music did not, and my fun time dwindled. I didn't feel like I was doing ministry; I just pushed buttons and watched dials.

Also, I conducted some careful statistical research, which showed this station didn't make a tremendous impact! After extensive planning, I pretended to get so engrossed in Monday Night Football in another room that I didn't put on the new program at the half hour. Since I slipped that one by with no phone calls, I pretended to forget again. When I finally woke up—I mean decided I'd gone far enough—and put something back on, there'd been 45 minutes of silence on the air: and nobody had noticed! I must have been involved in "What," because if the option is "Am I involved in ministry or what," I couldn't call this ministry!

Against this backdrop, I got...The Call.

When I got out of the Army, 22 years old, married, and with three children, Sweetie and I started attending First Big Church on the Corner. Eventually we found ourselves teaching 5th and 6th grade Sunday School and Junior Church, and enjoying life. First Big had a good youth pastor, with about 30 kids. We didn't bother them, and they didn't bother us. Our 5th & 6th graders looked forward to joining them, but it never crossed my mind. It was a good arrangement.

As youth pastors so often do however, this one left. The church found a suitable (?) replacement among the congregation, Mr. Lon G. Nuff. Lon was pretty good at knowing the Bible, but sometimes there is a strangely missing connection between knowing truth and expressing it. The class dwindled rapidly.

The Church—which means those Official People you're afraid of until you're one of them—asked me if I would be youth director. I think they'd held a meeting that went something like this:

"Has anyone noticed that since Lon started teaching the High School class dropped from 30 to 3?"

"No, but I like how quiet things are."

"We need to do something about this."

"Do we have to?"

"Yes, because we're a Church, and Churches have Youth Groups. If we have a Youth Group, then we can attract Young Families, and people will beat down the doors to attend here."

"Okay. But do we have to spend money?"

"I know, let's pray that God will send us someone who will do it for $800 a month. He's got to be married and have a family, so he won't go after the girls, and he has to keep a record of his time, so we know he puts in at least 40 hours a week! And if he hasn't gone to Bible College yet, let's make him go, but he's got pay for it himself."

(In unison) "Let's ask Ferd!"

"I don't know. Can we include custodial work in the $800?"

I wish there were archives with minutes from meetings like this, because I think I'm pretty close. It might be worth some money if I could prove it.

So I got the Call; or at least the Visit, because I didn't feel any call. "Ferd, we want you to be our new youth director (They didn't use the term 'youth pastor,' because it was beyond my humble status). We'll give you $800 a month, you'll keep records of your time, and go to Bible College. You will teach the High School Class, drive the Sunday School Bus, bring the Youth Group back up to 30, and do any other thing we might possibly decide is part of the job. You start Sunday!"

I was not overwhelmed by the offer. In fact, I wasn't whelmed at all, and didn't even pretend to be pseudo-whelmed. "Thanks, guys, but I'm just not worthy of such a prestigious position. Why don't you ask Clyde. He's been to Bible College, and he wants the job." It had never occurred to me that I might ever be called to 'ministry', and I think they were shocked to be turned down. But I seriously had no interest; and Clyde—sucker that he was—wanted to be youth director!

A short conversation ensued: "We don't want Clyde, we want you." "I don't want the job, hire Clyde." "We don't want Clyde, we want you." "I don't want the job, hire Clyde." A few repetitions and this got old, and we tabled the conversation for a while. In the meantime, I agreed to drive the bus and to teach the High School class. Once there I immediately reduced the attendance from three to one, losing the girl and her boyfriend who were there for reasons totally unrelated to either Sunday or school.

Follow my reasoning here: they want a class of thirty, I brilliantly produce a class of one. And they think I'm called to this? I tried. A missionary from Norway wanted me to take the kids skiing with him! Talk about a slam-dunk event! I called, sent letters, and settled in to watch the restoration of Youth Group. My only concern was protecting my ego from the ravages success. No one came. Absolute zero is not a temperature, it's a mood that proceeds from absolutely zero turnout at the big event that was guaranteed to succeed. I never did get even one of them to ever come back. You think I'm called to this?

Meanwhile, back at the station: the owner of KASH radio had received an offer he couldn't refuse. KASH was being sold and going secular. Horror of horrors. Who would have ever thought that KASH might some day not be Kristian? Having an immediate loss of job security at the same time the church was trying to get me to become youth director caused me to begin to recognize the wondrous workings of The Call.

Sweetie and I discussed: Let's see, as volunteers, she taught 5th & 6th grade Sunday School, I taught the High School class, or at least the High School boy.

We led Junior Church, and I drove the bus. As near as we could tell, the only thing missing from this picture was $800 and a title, and I was losing my job! I had always imagined that the Call involved peals of thunder and flashes of light, voices and things like that. My call seemed rather like a twisted arm by comparison, but you take what you can get.

Clyde, by the way, even though he thought he'd been called, never even received The Visit. Two things happened: First, he worked with me at Youth Group for a while. He had a lot of zeal and good ideas, and no hard feelings toward me. Second, he decided it had not been God's will for him to marry his wife in the first place, and he left her. Maybe the Church Board deserved more credit than I gave it.

One thing about The Call: It really was the call. No voice, no flash, no sudden burning desire or conviction. But I was a youth director/pastor for about four years, and I've been a pastor in recovery for almost 15 now. I think in real life, 'the call' comes as we are serving. Most of us simply realize we can be more effective if we have an official status, even if only 'youth director' because 'youth pastor' is too elevated for us. And, I was a lucky one. Many start at far less than $800 a month.

Youth Group Discipline

If you want to exercise church discipline, there are some scriptural passages you need to follow. You should look first at the instructions of Matthew 18, without forgetting the gentleness directed in Galatians 6. You can get more clarification and an example in I Corinthians 5. Church discipline can be very difficult and controversial. Youth Group discipline, on the other had, is very simple and straightforward. If you want to exercise Youth Group Discipline, just see me: I wrote the book.

In my group of around 30 kids, there were three who had parents in the church. The rest had little to no parental support, no church history—except for those who promoted up from Junior Church to Youth Group—and no idea of how to behave in church or Sunday School. Add to that the fact their leader was little better than them. Maybe worse (read on and judge for yourself). In the meantime, I had the challenge of maintaining discipline in my group.

For instance, what do you do with Rocky? Rocky grew up without many rules, and he was a fun loving kid. He lived near "The Dip" and had been an off-and-on member of the Group since Junior Church. He didn't have a mean bone in his body, just a thick bone on top of his body. Rocky didn't seem to get the difference between Okay Fun and Not Okay Fun, and often found himself in trouble. Because he was so good-natured, you couldn't get mad at him, you just wanted to straighten him out.

People were always leading Rocky to the Lord. Every time he got in trouble, he'd hang his head and be forlorn, and someone would decide "Rocky just needs the Lord." They would explain the plan of salvation to him, he would accept Jesus, and they would leave him alone. Rocky used it to avoid any serious consequences; but for all that leading, I don't think he ever found the Lord. If I had a nickel for every time Rocky got saved, I might have gained another month's salary.

One morning at Sunday School, the kids were unusually rowdy. Probably that jerk of a bus driver had taken them through The Dip a couple of times and got them worked up. The Dixon sisters were filling Sally in on the latest gossip, Amy and Cindy discussed the latest fashions, Lawrence, Jeff, and Jose were talking football, and Cam & Peter were all about TV wrestling. Everyone paid attention to someone other than me. I repeatedly tried to calm them down so they could be properly impressed by the brilliance of my lesson, but it wasn't going to happen.

Trying to keep calm, I drank water out of a plastic cup, counting to ten. Seventy. Seventy seven times. Finally, in frustration, I crushed the cup in my hand.

What a revelation! Eyes popped open, mouths popped shut, conversations stopped mid-syllable. "Oo, Ferd's mad." I couldn't figure it out. Because I crushed a plastic cup? Did they think it was glass? For whatever reason, though, they settled down and paid attention (though still somehow not impressed by my brilliance). They may not have learned much that day, but I did. If you want to establish Youth Group Discipline, threat of violence is highly effective!

Big Bob is the kind of kid I could relate to. Actually not that big, Bob was shorter than me, and I'm not 5'8"; but Bob thought big. A junior higher from my neighborhood, Big Bob rode the Sunday School bus. As the biggest kid on the bus, he naturally became king, and in his mind, this gave him the right to torment all the other kids. On just his second week on the bus, Big Bob pushed my last button.

Sweetie didn't ride the bus this day, which is too bad, because she could keep order with both the kids and with me. Today we had no protection. Bob was having a grand time harassing the kids and ignoring me. I'm sure he was thinking "What's he going to do? Stop the bus and come back and get me?" Bob should have remembered that I came from his neighborhood. I stopped the bus and came back to get him.

Hopefully you're already shaking your head in disbelief, thinking "You went back to get him?" Yes, get him. Get him as in do whatever it took to get his attention and straighten him out. As in be as physical as I felt I had to be. I'm not defending myself, just telling you what happened. Besides, compared to what I did to the kid at the skating rink, I was gentle with Big Bob.

My intention was to grab him by the front of his shirt, pull him eyeball to eyeball with me, and see if we could have a serious but short conversation. At the time I weighed 145: not a very intimidating picture. Bob, though shorter than me, probably equaled my weight. Doing the math as I walked back to him, I realized this demanded serious effort, because if I tried to move him and he didn't move, I would only create humiliation and misery for myself. Having figured this out, I prepared to give a mighty heave.

Bob, in the meantime, was no coward. I don't know what went through his mind, but he clearly wasn't afraid. He probably thought something like "This skinny little runt is coming after me?" In the true nature of a kid from my neighborhood, he stood to face me.

I learned two lessons that day: one in physics, and one in the deterrent effect of discipline. The physics lesson goes something like this: When an object that is exerting enough force to rise quickly to a standing position meets a force pulling hard enough to move that same object to a standing position, the combined exertion of force is enough to bounce said object's head off the ceiling of the bus.

The discipline lesson goes like this: when a bus full of rowdy kids sees the bus driver take the biggest and rowdiest kid on the bus and bounce his head off the bus ceiling, everyone, including said biggest and rowdiest kid, behaves himself remarkably well for the rest of the trip.

No lasting ill effects came from this incident, by the way. I doubt Bob ever told his parents, fearing he would get in trouble either for causing trouble on the bus, or more likely, for letting a little guy like me take him. He stayed and became a regular part of the group. I always thought of him as the member of the group most likely to go to jail (which he later did, but you can read about that in another chapter) and we got along just fine.

Now, about that kid at the skating rink. I never knew this kid, so I'll just call him 'This Kid,' 'That Kid,' or 'The Kid.' And while I never knew him, I'll never forget him.

I think Youth For Christ skate night is, or was, a universal thing used by Youth Groups all across America for decades; though I don't really know that for a fact. Skate Night became one of the best tools in my ministry, and helped establish my original group. All I had to do was publicize the night and drive the bus. And I didn't even have to prepare a lesson!

Skate Night also made a safe environment. Christian music played, everyone there came with a Youth Group, and you could pretty much relax, skate, and kibitz with other youth leaders. Normally, the most dangerous thing at Skate Night came when two of my girls and I played Crack the Whip during Triple Skate. Some evenings though, when there had been a school holiday, we would get kids who stayed from an earlier open skate session. This should be great; 'what an opportunity for ministry!' Nice theory. One kid who stayed this way was The Kid.

I've never been graceful at anything, but I know how to put out effort, and loved to go out for the "Speed Skate" session. The Kid was also a speed skater, faster and far more graceful than I. Apparently my skating was so bad it offended him, because at some point he came up behind me, pushed me, swore at me, and then skated on. Being a reasonable guy, and, don't forget, a Responsible Youth Group Leader, I decided to ignore him. In true Christian style, I 'turned the other cheek.' My but I'm a good Christian. My group sure is lucky to have me for a leader. A few laps later, This Kid came up behind me again, pushed me again, and swore at me again, then made a failed attempt to skate on again.

I say "failed" because fast and graceful as he was, he still couldn't skate with someone wrapped around his legs. Technically, I did a good job. It's not easy to tackle someone faster and more graceful than you while on skates. Then, while we were both sprawled on the floor, it occurred to me that he might try to hit me. I couldn't let that happen, so naturally I jumped on him and held him down. Since he was now my captive audience, I took the opportunity to explain to him in my gentlest screech that if he's going to shove and swear at people at Youth For Christ skate night, he should at least keep Christ's name out of it.

I'm not sure what the big deal was, but we somehow drew a crowd, and people—jumping to conclusions in that unreasonable way they have—seemed to think I was the one in the wrong! Sheepishly, I apologized to everyone, and skated over to the sidelines, where most of my kids sat in a group. I apologized to them, too, but they had heard him swear at me and seen him push me, and the only comment I got was "We were just surprised you didn't jump on him the first time!" No wonder I didn't have many discipline problems with my group.

The Bus

Driving a bus for Sunday School is very serious business. You want to have a thoroughly trained driver on a mechanically reliable bus, and you want to have a second adult on the bus to keep order. I know this because I'm able to learn from my mistakes.

In order to get the certification to drive a school bus today, you have to go through extensive and expensive state-run training. They don't want just any fool driving a bus. Back when I got my license, you could get your certification by going through your own church's driver training. They never told the church what to include in the training. Any Fool did get his license, and did drive a bus.

First Big did have a driver-training program. The driver I was replacing, let's call him 'Al,' put me in the driver's seat. "Start the bus," he said. Pretty tough; you turned the key and it started. It's good something went right. "Back out onto the street."

Did I tell you that First Big Church on the Corner sat on the corner of a busy downtown arterial? We didn't have a parking lot, we had a slab. It was just big enough for the bus to fit between the building and the sidewalk. To back the bus up you crossed the sidewalk, the parking spot, and moved into at least two lanes of oncoming traffic. We were also near two large hospitals, on a main ambulance route. While preaching the pastor had to learn to either pause for the sirens during his most dramatic points, or the congregation had to learn to read lips while he spoke and they heard "Woo-ooo Woo-ooo Woo-ooo" ("Mommy, how does he do that?"). First Big was also, as the name implies, a big building on a corner. The corner had a traffic light, and the building blocked the view of any cars that might be coming around that corner. You almost wished all cars had sirens. They're loud, but at least you know they're coming.

My first ever bus-driving experience required backing into this traffic. Fortunately, big yellow buses are big and yellow, and hard to miss; and no one wants to run into a Sunday School bus, because who are the police going to believe? For five years I backed the bus off the slab and into that traffic. Amazingly, I never ran into trouble (or anything else).

It's a good thing I had this good training, which I guess I should get back to. Al had me take a couple of lefts and a couple of rights, he had me drive up a hill and down a hill. The hills were nearby, we were back in 10 minutes. Al handed me a piece of paper with his signature on it and said "This is what you need to get your bus endorsement."

You might be surprised to learn the effect one piece of paper can have on some people. Al developed this barely controlled cackling problem as soon as he handed it over. He would lapse into it almost any time after that when he saw me. Sometimes I saw him first, and he would be fine until he noticed me, but when he did see me, the cackling began again. Poor guy.

That same piece of paper also had a unique effect on the lady at the licensing office. I don't know why they would put someone behind a counter who reacted to paper like that, but that's the government for you. As soon as I handed the slip over, her eyes went wide. You could see tension working it's way from her fingers up her arms, turning her whole body stiff. Obviously an allergic reaction. "Sir, have you been through a proper training course?" The words slurred a little, but I was proud of her for trying.

"Yes," I responded. "Al down at First Big was very thorough." While she had appeared tense before, she was now perfecting the art. A look of terror came over her, and I looked back to see what had come in the door, then I remembered the allergy. Poor girl; they really shouldn't make her handle paper.

She sent me on, my one good eye (bicycle wreck) passed the vision test, and I became a Legal School Bus Driver. As I left the building, I heard her starting to cackle.

The bus was one of my best friends in youth ministry. In fact, I found that as the kids got their own driver's licenses (a time when I myself would often become tense and develop a cackling problem) many would drop out of Youth Group. But until then, if someone was willing to offer them something to do and provide transportation to do it, they would be part of his Youth Group. Before long, my group grew to the required 30.

When you spend an hour on the bus before and after every church service and every youth event, you soon learn the short cuts. Taking the dip at the tracks saved about three blocks. The bus was old, the springs were sprung, and the shocks were shocking; all of which helped make The Dip the most popular place on the route. The squeamish gladly gave up their seats in the back, while the more daring started bouncing early, hoping to gain more airtime. Sometimes, just for fun, I would turn around and go through again. This wiped out the time-saving advantage of the short cut, but we sure had fun.

Another short cut, I only took once. The pastor's 13 year-old granddaughter stayed with him for the summer. Pastor Kahuna lived in a nice house in a nice neighborhood on a nice street. The street was actually two one-way streets, with a gently sloping paved canal for run-off between them. The proper way to take her home was to drive past his house about a quarter mile, make a U-turn at a bridge, and backtrack home. I decided to simply drive across that gentle dry canal and right into pastor's driveway. Highly superior. I wondered that I hadn't seen other people using this technique, but when you're exceptional like me, you get used to standing out in a crowd.

Did I say "gentle, paved canal?" It was; not at all like that rough dip at the tracks. But there was a little more slope to it than I thought. Enough that while the front of the bus was going up, the back still going down. The front bumper ground into the pavement in front and the back bumper ground into the pavement behind.

So there we were in this old bus, stuck in this nice neighborhood, with the words "First Big Church on the Corner" nicely stenciled on both sides of the bus, and right in front of the Pastor Kahuna's house. The trouble with being in trouble is you don't know if you want someone to notice or not. The kids' attitude didn't help, either. They pick the oddest times to have laughing fits.

Eventually, by shifting into 'Really Low' and playing with the steering wheel, we were able to get out. I had to drive the wrong way down a one-way street for about a quarter of a mile, until I could turn around at this bridge. Then I just backtracked to the pastor's house, and dropped his granddaughter off, so my shortcut worked after all.

Still on the subject of dips, but not of short-cuts, I got a phone call from the police one snowy morning. Someone reported that I had been letting kids ski-jog the bus at The Dip. The funny thing is, I was innocent. It's not that I wouldn't have done that kind of thing, I just hadn't thought of it! The officer did a really good job of describing us: an old bus with the words "First Big Church on the Corner" stenciled on the sides, towing kids through the dip. Being of a keen detective mind, I offered proof of my innocence: "Come look at the snow on the slab. The bus hasn't been driven." My keen detective mind has also come up with a likely suspect for the false report: Rocky lived right next to the dip—I think he was trying to plant the idea in my mind.

A curious side-effect of being bus driver—it also made me bus mechanic. I hope you're laughing now; if there is anything funny in this book this is it. I didn't even own any left handed screwdrivers. One of the men in the church, Let's call him 'Mr. Lodge,' taught mechanics at the community college, and when the bus needed work he would seat me in the engine compartment, stand nearby, and tell me what to do. He couldn't get over the fact that I didn't have any left-handed screwdrivers, but what can I do? I'm right-handed.

One of the more repetitive problems with an old bus is the curse of the dead battery, but that's not really a problem when you've got a manual transmission and a Youth Group. You just call out "Group Push!" and you're started. On one occasion, most of the group went to another activity, and I didn't have enough with me to push the bus. No problem! We called them, they came and pushed, and we all went home.

The bus started to develop a funny knock, bad enough that it even caught my attention. I pointed it out to Mr. Lodge, who I think is somewhat devious. He said, "Don't worry, just drive it." Driving home it threw a rod. Then Mr. Lodge and I got to enjoy a church sponsored field trip to another city to buy a newer bus. The only one in our price range short enough to fit on the slab had a lift for handicapped access. We bought it, disabled the lift, and mounted a seat there. It became one of the most popular seats on the bus.

I parked the bus on the street in front of my house. In some neighborhoods this might be a problem, but not in ours. In fact, it added a certain ambiance when set off against the Tattoo Parlor across the street. Besides, the bus looked at least as good as the cars we drove. It kept the Jehovah's Witnesses away, too. One day we did get a visit from a couple of Christian gentlemen doing door to door evangelism.

"Do you know Jesus Christ as your Savior?"

"Yes I do. You see that bus out there? The one that says 'First Big Church on the Corner'? I drive that bus."

"That's nice. But have you trusted Jesus Christ for salvation?"

"Yes I have. I'm Youth Director and teach Junior Church over at First Big"

"That's nice. But if you died tonight…"

I appreciate their dedication and zeal, but somehow I found them offensive. I would rather have the Jehovah's Witnesses or Mormons come to my door, at least I can argue with them. And, it seems, they respected the bus.

I never hit a kid on the bus (Except Big Bob, but that's another chapter), but I once hit a dog with the bus. It was one of those rare occasions that we actually had a mom on the bus. I think, aside from Sweetie, we only had three moms and one Grandma that ever rode the bus in over five years of driving it. One of them found Christ, and is serving Him today. Something put the fear of God into her—I hope it wasn't the bus ride.

This particular day, there were some new kids on the bus, who lived on an unpaved street. The Dumbest Dog in the World lived on their block. We dropped them off, arranged to get them next week, and left. All of a sudden the rear end took a huge lift, and I wondered how I could have not seen such a huge pothole. Looking in the mirror, there was something in the street.

It was a perfectly beautiful but perfectly dead husky. Long on looks, short on brains. I knocked on some doors and found a neighbor who said "It's about time. That dumb dog is always chasing cars. The owners aren't home, I wouldn't worry about it." As near as I can tell, the dog had the habit of chasing cars, which are both shorter and faster than the bus. It ran after the bus in it's usual car chasing position, which would place it right behind your normal car, but put it right in front of a bus's back tire.

It wasn't my fault, and I feel no guilt, but when I climbed back on the bus, 4 year old John, son of Mom Who Was On The Bus, said through his tears: "Ferd, why did you murder that dog?" I'm really glad mom was on the bus to comfort him, but I know John never thought of me the same way again. And I think Mom had her doubts, too.

The day finally came when my status changed from 'Bus Driver' to 'Recovering Bus Driver.' I still remember my feeling of satisfaction. I had an hour drive to The Little Church Down the Road, where they were foolishly considering me for pastor (I decided not to tell them they should just consider me for 'director'). Sunday School at Little Church started at the same time as at First Big. The new driver for First Big had to come to our house to get the bus, and he left half an hour before we did. I waved goodbye with a cup of coffee in my hand, relaxed for 30 blessed minutes, then left, arriving at Little Church in time. I can live with this.

My driver's license now has an endorsement that says "Organ Donor," but no endorsement for a bus. I've learned where to draw the line.

Never Assume

It's difficult to describe how much I couldn't do things people assumed I could do. Their expectations might have made sense if I'd actually applied for the job and said I knew anything. But they came to me! Remember? I was honest—I didn't claim to know anything (You don't get more honest than that!). They had actually seen me teach Junior Church using flannelgraphs. Without any assistance whatsoever from me, they made a leap to the conclusion that I would therefore make a good youth director. Talk about a blind leap of faith. All it meant was that I knew how to use a flannelgraph.

Early on, Pastor Kahuna asked me to do an object lesson for the kids in front of the whole church. I guess he wanted to introduce me to the congregation in my new role. I'm not given to fears, but this scared me to death. I had this huge burning question I didn't know how to ask: "What's an object lesson?"

Somewhere along the way, I've learned that if you don't know something the thing to do is "Ask," but I hadn't learned that concept yet. Seriously. I thought there were things you were just supposed to know, and since you were supposed to know, it was wrong to admit you didn't know. I can best illustrate this disability of mine by telling you how I used to work on my car.

At 17, I bought a car for $20. It was a good car and worth every penny. Not being a total ignoramus, I knew spark plugs had to be changed every so often, and that they were supposed to have something called a "gap." No one had ever told or shown me how to set a gap, resulting in the curious circumstance that I didn't know how. Since real men know how to do this stuff, I couldn't ask and expose myself as less than a real man! Fortunately, I was able to redeem myself and prove I'm a real man by trying to figure it out without asking. I took the old spark plugs out, screwed the new ones in tight, and then unscrewed them just a little, creating a gap (In case you were thinking of trying this technique, I now advise against it). I changed spark plugs a lot in that car; for some reason they always seemed to be faulty. I wonder how much money I might have saved on spark plugs if I'd ever "asked" how to gap them, but there's that word again. If that doesn't illustrate my disability well enough, sometime I'll tell you about the time I plopped an alternator on the counter and told the parts man "I need a starter."

For fear of looking like a fool, I wouldn't ask questions I perceived as foolish; guaranteeing I remained a fool.

So here I was, the new Youth Director, who of course knew simple things, like "how to do good object lessons for kids in front of the whole church." But I'd never heard the words "object" and "lesson" used in the same sentence in my life, and I didn't know how to ask questions.

It got down to three or four days, and Pastor K. seemed to think this an easy task, so I stayed calm. I can figure this thing out! Yeah, right. Do you know how hard it is to figure out even obvious things when you're clueless? Try these on: Maybe an object lesson is a lesson people will obviously object to, like playing the devil's advocate. Maybe there are these certain things they call "objects" that every pastor knows about, and you go to the object shelf at the pastor store, and they tell you how to give a lesson. Maybe it's as far out as taking an everyday object, and you apply Scripture to it to teach a biblical truth.

By Friday, I became so desperate I actually admitted to Pastor K. I didn't know what an object lesson is. He gave me that confused, awkward kind of look that makes you want to check your fly. Like I'd just asked the question in Swahili. His look said "I heard the question, but you can't really be asking what an object lesson is, so I don't know what you're asking." Then he said, "You use an object to teach a lesson. It's easy, you can do it."

Well, that's progress. Now I had a definition. Still, I couldn't remember ever seeing one done, and didn't feel much better. What I finally did was grab my old combat boots. take them to the front of church, and say "These are my old combat boots. They remind me of an old Russian story of the bootmaker who was told Jesus was going to visit..." It wasn't a real object lesson, but it seemed to go over okay.

I did learn something out of that experience. I'm not the only person who doesn't know things he ought to know. On the way out of church, an older couple stopped me. The gentleman shook my hand and said "I really enjoyed that. That's always been one of my favorite stories from the Bible." Their ignorance surprised me. I could have taught them a lot if they'd only asked.

Pastor K. had a real knack for telling me to do things I didn't know how to do.

"I want the kids to sing a special for church in two weeks. I'd like to see you lead them."

"I'd like to see that too, Pastor K., but we've never done that kind of thing before, the kids might not want to do it, I don't know if any of us has any talent, and I've never led any kind of singing in my life." "Lead" and "Singing" were another two words I'd never heard in the same sentence before.

"I'm sorry, Ferd; let me rephrase: The kids will sing in church in two weeks, and you will lead them."

"Oh, now I understand."

I went to the Christian bookstore, and discovered accompaniment tapes. I found one I thought the kids might like, and told them in my best positive voice "We've got to get practicing. In two weeks we're singing this for the church!" Amazingly, they didn't like the idea. "We've never done this kind of thing before, we don't have any talent, and we've never sung in public in our lives!" Have I ever told you about my gift of prophecy?

They were good kids, though, and gave it their best shot. Two weeks later they did a heroic job of dealing with stagefright while singing a poorly led and poorly practiced song to a congregation that didn't appreciate it but complained that it was "too rocky." Naturally, Pastor K. asked us to do it again. We didn't improve with practice, and finally got a break.

Probably my worst experience of all came when Pastor K told: "Have some of the kids share their testimonies at evening service tonight." You have to assume at least three things to make that statement: 1. The completely untrained youth director has taught the kids how to share a testimony, 2. That the kids he's scavenged freshly from the neighborhood have a testimony to share, and, 3. That the kids will be willing to stand in front of church and share it. All three of these assumptions were beyond our group.

Had someone ever told me "Ferd, you should teach the kids how to share their testimonies," I'd have seen the reason in that, and complied. If you think it's miserable that I hadn't already done that, you're wrong. Miserable is how I felt having to have it done "by tonight." You might assume any youth director would know these things, but it's surprising how much a person can not know.

The second assumption above is the saddest, but true. I didn't know at all which of my kids might have a testimony to share. I taught the gospel and the kids had all heard their need to take Jesus to be your Savior. But I didn't seem to be able to ask for a response. What makes this so serious is most of these were not "church kids." There was no family training, support, or encouragement, so if they didn't get it from me, they didn't get it. But I was afraid of making some uncomfortable or driving them away, so I treated them all as if they had already accepted Christ. As a result I didn't have much of a clue who had and who had not.

So I stood in front of this group of maybe saved kids who've never been talked to about their testimonies before and asked: "Who would like to share their testimonies at Evening Service tonight?" It was probably a lot like asking them to do an object lesson or lead singing. I knew I was asking them to do what I didn't know they could do, but Pastor Kahuna had said I would have some kids share their testimonies that night, so by golly, I'd better have some kids share their testimonies that night. They didn't seem eager to cooperate.

Getting no response at all, I softened it: "Maybe someone can share how Jesus is working in their lives today?" A couple of the girls had recently had an adventure where they'd been chased through a parking lot by a strange man. They managed to share that story, and worked into it that Jesus had protected them. I stood at the back of the room, and tried to act proud, but I was dying inside.

The one thing Pastor K. never did ask me to do for evening service was a flannelgraph lesson. Too bad, that's something I could have done.

Special Rules for Girls

Every man who has entered youth ministry knows there are special rules that apply to the girls, but no one ever tells you what they are! I believe this is because, until now, no one has either been brave enough, or foolish enough. One way or the other, I'm qualified to tell.

When God gave the ten commandments, He gave them to a man, and ten were enough. But as every youth worker knows, girls are special, so I give you twenty.

1. Never yell at a 14 year girl playing catcher on your church softball team to "pick up the ball." Even though you're not really yelling at her but just saying "Pick up the ball," in a loud voice, she will not understand and will burst into tears. She doesn't know that "there is no crying in baseball." She will not pick up the ball, the runner will score, you will blow your lead and lose the game, and everyone will think you're a big jerk.

2. Never arm wrestle a girl, even when she's bigger than you and you still know you can beat her. After she realizes you are toying with her she will use both arms and legs and everything else and throw all her weight into it. It will wrench your arm and really hurt.

3. When you find out one of the girls is going on camping trips with her boyfriend and his family, and she says "Don't worry, his parents are there and nothing can happen," worry anyway.

4. Never, when a girl says she was flattened, respond by saying "You don't look flat to me."

5. When you're driving someplace very far, like on a mission trip, and one of the girls says she has to go to the bathroom, Listen to her. Even if you're not

the driver, it might be a good idea to intercede for her. She probably really has to go.

6. Never allow girls to wear two piece swimsuits when going to the water slides. You never know when she will decide to stop in a tube and surprise you, or if when you come barreling into her at full speed, your big toe might lodge in the wrong place and rip her top off. Should this happen, you will come tumbling out of the tube together in a highly embarrassing tangle, trying to help her cover herself while not seeing anything yourself. If you are lucky, she will get the thing back on before too many people realize what happened.

7. If you are playing Capture the Flag, and you and one of the girls are trying to pull each other out of no man's land into your own territory, and you see her 6'4" brother running to her aid, you should never panic and give in to the desperate urge to give one last mighty tug. You might just pull so hard that you launch her right past you, and she cracks her knee violently on that big rock you didn't notice, and everyone will think you're a big jerk.

8. Never be first to respond when you hear a girl screaming at a retreat. If she's got a bee up her blouse, there's nothing you can do to help..

9. Never yell at a girl because she worked ahead and finished the devotional material you designed to be done over a period of weeks. She was really proud and now you've hurt her feelings, you big jerk.

10. If you have a pretty girl in your group who lives near the red light district, and whose parents never leave the porch light on because it's burnt out and they just haven't gotten around to replacing it, you should never, after dropping the rest of the kids off, remember that you were going to get her a replacement bulb at church, and go back into the empty, dark church alone with her to get it. As soon as you get to the closet, you will realize how this looks, but it's too late to do anything about it now. Even though it's totally innocent and nothing happened, you will feel paranoid for months wondering when someone is going to bring it up and question what you were up to. Even years later, when she is happily living in Idaho with her husband and three children, you will wonder how you could ever have done anything so stupid.

11. If your youth group has been playing in a body of water near a busy highway, and one of the girls wants to change into something dry and you tell her

"Change in the back of the van (which has tinted windows)." Make sure she understands you. It doesn't do you much good to make all the guys turn their backs to the van until she's finished only to learn she changed out in back of the van. Your group won't see her, but for a short time, traffic will slow considerably on the highway.

12. If you are playing Caveman Football, make sure the older guys know better than to plow over the smaller girls like Patriot missiles hunting scud rockets. Even though the only person I've ever known to get hurt playing the game was myself (cracked rib), it looks bad to the parents when their daughters go home still wondering what hit them. Girls are delicate and fragile, and prefer to get knocked down more nicely.

13. If you are jumping off a 40 foot rock into a lake, and the girl about to jump has never done it before, make sure she knows to keep her legs together and her arms at her side. Otherwise she's likely to hit the water all spread out, and have painful red marks on the inside of her arms and legs. Even though she loved it and climbs back up to jump again, you look like a big jerk. That's all you need after you yelled at her to pick up that softball.

14. When parents call you at a late hour of the night, wanting to know why you haven't brought their daughter back from the Youth Group outing yet, and you didn't have a Youth Group outing that night, find their daughter and drag her home. Especially if it was Clyde trying to have a special event with a few select young people, and he didn't clue you in. You mess up enough things on your own, you don't need his help.

15. Call ahead when you are bringing someone's daughter home two hours late.

16. When you come home and the aroma of coffee is so strong it almost knocks you over before you even get out of the car, and you find two of the girls thought they would make themselves at home and "Wouldn't it be nice if we had some coffee for Ferd and Sweetie when they got here?" Don't come unglued. After all, it was only two cups of coffee out of your $800/month salary, and they were trying to be nice. They didn't even know you were so poor you recycled the few grounds you did use.

17. If one of the girls is riding in the car with you and your family, and because there isn't much room one of your young sons is sitting on her lap, and she didn't get the door completely shut so when you go around a corner the door

flies open and your son rolls out right into a downtown intersection, you should first make sure your son is okay, but after that it is okay to hug the screaming girl. Do not be afraid to do so just because you have been warned against showing physical affection. If you fail to hug her when she needs it like this, you will be aware for at least the next 15 years that you should have. and you will feel like a big jerk.

18. If you are going to let the girls use your ties as a fashion statement, Say goodbye to the ties. Do not bother trying to get them back. Even if you do, they will not be in a wearable condition.

19. If you decide to play Slug Bug with a girl you are driving home in your car, be sure you are man enough to take it. She may be a lot tougher than you think. She's a little more solid than when you arm-wrestled her.

20. If you ever get depressed thinking of all the ways you've blown it so many times, you should pull out the photo album and live a while in your memories. Organize your photo album properly: while events are fresh, arrange your album by events, for the kids to look at. After a couple of years, arrange your album by the individuals, for you to look at. On the page that features the 14 year old catcher and rock-jumper, you may also see her wedding picture, her pretty daughter, and her twins. It will remind you that while you failed many times and in many ways, you succeeded in building a relationship of love.

The Youth Group Cookbook

SPAGHETTI

1. Kill Cow
2. Skin Cow
3. Grind everything left into hamburger
4. Add tomato sauce....

There are many people out there who function according to the absurd premise that quality is more important than quantity. Of course, there will always be amateurs, but why so many of them? I guess we should just accept the truth—very few people who work with youth groups make it past amateur status, being unable to adapt to reality and move beyond absurd premises in the face of hard facts. Quality is no issue. Junior and Sr. High kids rarely slow down enough to taste food; the only issue is whether you can offer enough to satisfy them.

Many people who have worked with teens and think they know a thing or two believe that nothing in the world eats more than a teen-age boy. They're close. Admittedly, it's an awesome sight to watch a couple of the big boys go at it. They can shovel away so much food that you want to get out your encyclopedia and turn to that page where they show the inner organs of the human body, knowing there must be other chambers than the stomach for that kind of volume. I personally have a theory that no organs but the stomach develop to more than pea size until the late teen years. All the room these organs will someday occupy are in the meantime designated storage areas.

In addition to how much they can eat at any given time, you have to allow for the fact that they can eat that much all the time. Youth worker Albert Onestone developed his famous formula of dietary relativity to describe it: $e=mc24$ (eating = meals x candy 24 hours a day).

Still, if you want to be impressed by volume of eating, it's a mistake to look at the Senior High boys; football players and such. The ones to watch are the Junior

High girls. The thing about these girls is no matter how experienced you are and how many times you've seen it, they still catch you by surprise. They're such petite dainty things, like hummingbirds. And, like hummingbirds, they daily consume an amount equal to or greater that their body weight.

I remember the mother who came into youth group in a slightly dazed condition. She had given her daughter and a few of her friends a ride to youth group, and stopped by McDonalds on the way. To my horrified cry of "You didn't let them order what they wanted!" she let her wide eyes wander around the room for a second or two, before rallying enough to turn her blank face in my direction and force a syllable, "Yes."

I helped her into a dark, cool room and had her sit down. When I came out, I saw she had left her purse, but that didn't matter, it would be empty anyway. They'd had to stock up at a convenience store between McDonald's and the church, which was guaranteed to wipe out whatever cash she had left. Sometimes it's even been known to result in debit card meltdown. By this time her daughter was now going through the kitchen cupboards, looking for what she might find.

Back to the Spaghetti. Sweetie had decided to cut the recipe somewhat, using something less than a cow. Still, there was a large roasting pan full to the top with this sauce that smelled truly delicious (I'll never know how it tasted). The biggest pot we could lay our hands on sat next to it, full of noodles. The kids lined up, and waited for the blessing—in youth group-ese 'amen' means 'go'—and I could tell a little instruction was needed. "Those of you in front, be sure you leave enough for everyone else."

To the typical teen, "enough for everyone else" means "Don't take more than half." Before we knew what was happening, the first in line took half, number two took half of what was left. I started to yell something about being considerate of others, but sound doesn't travel that fast. Their plates were empty, and they were eyeballing the back of the line, wondering how they could hold off starvation until they could get seconds. "What's for dessert?"

COFFEE

3/4 cup milk

1/4 cup sugar

Add a touch of warm, brown liquid for effect, preferably decaffeinated

Drinking coffee is a right of passage, and new Jr. Highers want to prove they're mature, just like the rest of the group. "Do your parents let you drink coffee at home?" "Yeah, I drink coffee all the time. I love coffee."

"You let Junior High kids drink coffee?" Relax, rookie. A Junior Higher is as likely to drink coffee as your cat is to jump in the lake. He just wants you to know he's old enough to drink coffee if he wants to. So let him. In fact, force the issue. Mount a hidden video camera somewhere to catch the whole thing, it might be worth some money.

Jr. Higher: "Are you drinking coffee?"

Responsible Adult Youth Worker: "Why yes, would you like some?"

Jr. Higher: "Yes, I think I would."

Responsible Adult Youth Worker: (Move quickly, before Junior Higher can stop you) "Here let me pour you a cup." (Fill it up, leaving no room for added ingredients.)

Jr. Higher: (Through puckered lips) "Mmm. This sure is good coffee. But it's kind of hot. I need to cool it down a little." (He quickly moves to sink, pouring most of the contents down the drain.) "Where's the milk?"

Responsible Adult Youth Worker: "We don't have any. We just have some of those little creamers."

Jr. Higher: "Only seven! Don't you have any more?"

Responsible Adult Youth Worker: (Knowing there's plenty in the cupboard) "Sorry, that's about it."

Jr. Higher: "I guess it'll have to do, then. What about sugar?"

Responsible Adult Youth Worker: "That's the white stuff in that cup right in front of you."

Jr. Higher: (Five spoonfuls later, sipping from a cup of gooey white stuff, slightly warmer than ice:) "Mmm, just the way I like it."

Don't worry, he'll never ask for coffee at Youth Group again. He just had to show you he's a man.

PROGRESSIVE BANANA SPLIT

1. Four houses with parents too inexperienced to know better
2. At First house, Maraschino Cherries
3. At Second house, nuts
4. At third house, bananas and flavored syrups

5. At fifth house, ice cream, flavored syrups, and all the toppings already listed

6. Assorted dilapidated getaway vehicles

There are several reasons to do a progressive banana split, probably the least of which is that it is fun. The best reasons are that the host homes will usually provide their portion of the banana split, and then they are stuck with the clean-up (Which is why you want those dilapidated getaway vehicles to be quick. You can use the bus if you want; you won't outrun anyone, but you can knock them off the road.).

Start at the church with empty bowls. No toppings, no spoons, no anything else. Withholding spoons won't prevent the kids from eating as they go, but it does prevent spoon loss.

Be sure to have the kids RSVP for the event. Theoretically, this will ensure you have enough car space, but teens universally believe RSVP means Rignore initials you don't understandSVP, so this attempt at control will fail. Just divide the kids so that each of the dilapidated vehicles are equally overloaded.

Only use vehicles in a poor state of repair, because only a fool or a madman would use his nice vehicle to ferry teenagers on a progressive banana split. Youth workers often are fools and madmen, but you will need to acquire additional volunteer drivers. Suitable vehicles are not hard to find; just find someone who has previously held a progressive banana split. They will be glad to let you drive their vehicle, since it has lost all resale value.

When you arrive at the first house, the host will naturally be disappointed at the poor turn out, since you told him to expect about three times that number. Don't let him know that you knew exactly how many were coming. You have to pad the numbers (the same way you do when you tell how much time you spend in prayer), or he will never buy enough Maraschino Cherries. Some adults really think you can limit teens to two or three! Maybe two or three per swallow. I personally have never seen more than seven in a bowl at one time, though I'm sure the seven in a bowl were the remainder of a much larger take from the jar (coincidentally, by a Jr. High girl).

Whatever the number of Maraschino Cherries put in the bowl at the first house, none will arrive at the second house. Most won't make it as far as the car. Those that do will find a way to become lodged in some visible but unreachable part of the interior.

This scene repeats itself from house to house, the script remains exactly the same except for the ingredients, until you reach the last house. At the last house, you have all the makings of enough banana splits for a group three times your number. Never mind that the group has already averaged 6 Maraschino Cherries, 2 bananas, half a cup of crushed walnuts and 8 ounces of assorted syrups each; you don't dare cheat these kids out of their complete Banana Splits. By this time they are so hyper they are capable of anything.

At each house along the way you play a short game or sing songs. Games aren't necessary for the kids, but hosts recognize they're just being used if you only eat and run. Games should be short enough to get the kids out before they damage anyone's house. Leave quickly enough that you're out before the host realizes that yes, his house is damaged. In addition to being short, they must be simple. Games that require any level of concentration will be a mistake.

You have a message prepared for the last house. Do not try to make it deep, unless, like me, you are expert enough to pull it off. I personally wowed them last time with my lesson on the Rapture: "Will You Be Talking With Your Mouth Full When the Big Banana Splits?" Many youth leaders are not up to this kind of serious study however, and it's not really necessary. Your goal with this event is to attract new kids to your group, and revive interest among those who are losing it. Some of them will show up for your next regular meeting, and you can impress them with your depth then.

FRUIT OF THE SPIRIT

Take the milk of human kindness, season it with the salt of the earth, liberally add God's Word, which is sweeter than honey, and the honeycomb. Serve with the Bread of Life and Living Water. Tenderize, and prepare without leaven. Mix without shaking or beating.

This recipe takes a great deal of time to prepare, and must be continually mixed as long as you know them, but is worth it. This dessert will satisfy. Both the kids and you will rejoice in your just desserts.

The Don'ts of Mission Trip

I know what you're thinking, it's supposed to be "The Do's And Don'ts of Mission Trip," but I don't want to go beyond the level of my expertise. And I'm really good at the don'ts.

In 1988 the World's Fair was going on in Vancouver, B.C. Mr. Lodge talked to me about taking the kids on a mission trip, with a trip to the fair thrown in. "What a great idea!" I thought. "We'd never see it any other way, and we can do a VBS, teach our kids, help some other church, and reach other kids all at the same time!" So we put the wheels in motion, and pulled together our Mission Trip. Being new at this, I made a few tiny mistakes. Here are a few don'ts you don't want to do.

1. Don't make your kids eat worms.

We announced at church we would love to tackle any work projects we could handle for donations toward the trip. One lady had wanted to remove the sod from the strip between her sidewalk and the curb and put in a rock garden, so she hired us to do the work. I took three guys, and off we went.

Here we were, pulling up sod, when Cameron up and says "I've eaten a worm before."

"That's nice," I said. "Go empty the wheelbarrow."

Two minutes later, Cam repeats himself, "Really guys, I ate a worm before."

"We don't care, Cam. Take this piece of sod."

"No, really guys, I ate a worm before!"

Suppose you are the Responsible Youth Worker. You are a rock. You are able to overlook all kinds of openings and opportunities. It's a good thing you are, because I'm not.

We were pulling up sod, for crying out loud. With all sorts of big, fat, juicy worms right in front of us? I restrained myself, using all my self-control, and didn't grab the scrawny little worm in front of me and tell him to eat it. Not me. Instead I waited until I found a really big fat one.

"Okay Cam, prove it." I dangled the big, fat, juicy worm in front of him. Back and forth, up and down. I was about to reel in a sucker.

"With that?"

"Yep."

"Now?"

"Yep."

"Do I have to?" You'd almost think he didn't want to eat the worm.

"Unless you're a liar." I grinned.

He tried to wipe a little bit of the dirt off, but it's harder than you might think. Finally, he held it up, opened his mouth, and ate it. In a few minutes we excused him and finished the work without him. Most of the sod was up by then anyway.

2. Don't make rules if you don't know why you have them.

"No walkmans, tape players, handheld electronic games, etc." Every Youth Worker has enforced non-electric gadget rules since Ben Franklin's youth group leader told him to stop playing with that kite and key. Since everyone else uses these rules, I did too. Why do you have this rule? Well, because it's a good rule. What a dumb question! Everyone knows that! And besides, "Those things disrupt group unity."

Let's think about it. We're going to ride a bus together for a long time. We all know each other, and are already friends. We've been preparing for months for this trip and are a well-prepared team. And a walkman is going to destroy all this?

Somehow, some of the kids didn't see the logic behind this rule, and chose to ignore it. I, being the layer down of the law, didn't see the logic behind the rule either, but it was always a rule for all groups, so it must be upheld. Being thus persuaded, I determined to enforce The Rule.

After only one or two hours of exciting and adventure-filled hours of highway monotony, I noticed Lawrence happy and content in one of the back seats. Why did he seem so satisfied when everyone else was clearly bored? He must be breaking a Rule! Ahh, He's listening to an evil walkman! Filled with righteous rage, I stormed back and demanded the vile machine.

"Why?" He asked innocently.

"Because it's an evil machine and it threatens to destroy our group unit."

He took a quick look at the bored faces scattered throughout the bus—"Huh?"

"And it's a Rule, so hand it over!"

Eventually my logic overwhelmed him, and he handed over the sinister device. Having already put on my sterile rubber gloves, I carefully dropped it into a protective baggy, promising to return it when the trip was over. That was the first, I acquired one or two more before the ride was over.

For some reason I couldn't understand, my actions seemed to disrupt group unity. In fact they almost resulted in group mutiny! But I had succeeded to some extent, the group seemed unified in tension, boredom, and resentment for the rest of the ride.

The story is not over, though, I had only won Round One. Round Two began after we arrived at our destination and I realized the sinister sound systems were gone from the glove box. Getting the attention of the group, I made an announcement: "I have decided Walkmans are okay, so long as you don't use them during group activities. The way I figure it now, when I won Round One, everyone lost, and when I lost Round Two, everyone won.

3. Don't stay at different places.

Speaking of group unity, there is no group unity when there is no chance for group unity. Members of the church we worked at graciously offered to keep members of our team in their homes. These people were all extremely gracious. I remember the very nice homes and the tremendous meals they showered on us. I don't know if I have ever experienced such hospitality anywhere else. But a scattered group cannot function as a unit.

We depended on our hosts for rides to and from the church each day. That meant we didn't get there in time to organize for devotions, or even a group prayer. Every day after VBS there was a fun activity for the kids. Again, no time to be alone as a group. During the whole week, we didn't have one group devotions or prayer time together, except at the start and finish of the trip.

4. Don't go to a church that doesn't need you.

I had this misconception that we were going to a small, struggling church somewhere on the outskirts of Vancouver that needed help to put on VBS. I told the kids, "This is real ministry, because we're going to a small, struggling church somewhere on the outskirts of Vancouver that needs help to put on VBS." I was just a little off.

I'm trying to think of the one word that best describes this church. "Dynamic" comes to mind. "Big" doesn't say enough. "Thriving" might be close. Maybe the best way to say it is that we arrived at a really good church. We came from a church with a big name, and a big building, but it wasn't a big church. It wasn't an exciting church. And we arrived to "Help" a church that was everything ours wasn't?

We started our week at the church by joining their upbeat Sunday evening service. The good music, full sanctuary, and dynamic message thrilled the group but sobered me. One question rose from every teen after the service: "What's wrong with our church?"

Here's a dilemma you don't want to face: You want the best for your youth group, and your church isn't it! It gave them a hunger for what I couldn't give them, but agreed they should have.

As it turns out, the church must have had some problems. Like, why does a big, active church like that want a youth group from far away to come put on VBS for them? I think part of it was ministry—to let our kids have a chance to see the world's fair—and I'm grateful, but we didn't really get to do what we came to do, which was to share the gospel with kids who needed Christ. We did put on VBS, along with their youth group and one of their pastoral staff, but it felt more like baby-sitting church kids than reaching the lost. Some churches are small enough that they really do need help to reach their community, but this wasn't one of them. They should have done it themselves.

Regardless, our kids went away seeing the failings of First Big in a new light. They saw what church can be, and First Big looked pretty small.

5. Don't leave discipleship out of the training

I used an interesting recruiting approach for the trip: "We're going to Vancouver for the World's Fair, and to do a VBS. Who wants to help?" It's a good way to get hands raised, but not the right way. Scripture makes it clear those who are faithful in small things will be faithful in big things; those who are faithful with what they have will be trusted with more; teachers will be judged more strictly, you should not lay hands on anyone too quickly…Naturally I bypassed all that. My standard was substandard: "Are you willing to do this work in Jesus' name so you can go to the World's Fair?"

We immediately started training for the trip. The kids learned how to do puppets, how to lead songs, how to lead a child to Christ (some of them needed to be led, not to lead), how to do crafts. They specialized according to their gifts and abilities: One emcee, one songleader, a couple of game leaders, one flannelgraph storyteller, and so on. I can say this about our group—they were well prepared in the mechanics of Vacation Bible School.

Somehow I missed the need to spend time with them on their personal walk with Christ. I guess I thought training in these things was discipleship, and that by learning these things they would be deepening their walk with Christ. How foolish. I knew better. I'm one of those guys who sometimes calls seminary 'cemetery;' I knew that learning does not make you godly, even back then. But I didn't ask for any kind of Bible reading or personal devotions. I didn't check on their prayer lives, I never asked them "How's your walk with Christ going?" The kids were well prepared with the mechanics for ministry, but not with the heart for ministry.

6. Don't go home.

The group never recovered from this mission trip. We returned to find things had turned for the worse at First Big. The kids had come home thinking their church had problems, only to find things were worse than they thought. They became even more disillusioned with the church than they already were. They needed me more than ever, and I had no time. I was in my senior year of Bible college, was Youth Pastor, and for a while, after Pastor Kahuna left under pressure, Interim Pastor. Don't forget I still drove the bus and taught Sunday School. And, oh yeah, I was married with three children; I think two of them were boys.

When anyone asked me about the mission trip, I talked about the positives. From the outside it looked great—we did lots of fun things, saw lots of new places—but in my honest opinion, nothing went well. That's why I don't know how to do a mission trip—I only know how not to.

Help!

Help is a word that can be used so many ways. Help can be used as a noun to describe those who help. In that case "HELP!" would mean 'I'm so excited about all the quality help I got when I was youth director at First Big!' Help can also be a one word sentence, requesting assistance. In that case, "HELP!" would mean 'I'm way over my head here. Will someone please come and bail me out.' In my case, "HELP" is a cry for assistance from those who would have liked to be quality helpers, but couldn't get that lunk to recognize he was way over his head and needed to be bailed out.

Sweetie was always my best help. She's always understood me, and still bails me out regularly. In addition to that, she made this vow before God and man, and being a godly woman, she's obligated. Every man who wants to "go into ministry"' like this needs a Sweetie, because everyone else, when they realize how dense and stubborn you are, will eventually bail on you. Also, I'm willing to admit I need her.

My first other help was Clyde. Clyde was a real asset to a guy like me when starting out, because he had a clue. (I had a game at home called Clue, which is good, because otherwise I'd have been Clueless.)

Clyde wasn't real big on some of the larger things, which built the group in numbers, but he was very interested in discipleship and teaching. He knew publishers and materials, and understood a variety of teaching techniques. In some ways, I was probably more of a front man for him than the one running the program. That's a good thing. Because I sure didn't know what program to run!

He understood we needed a core group within the larger group. A core group is the group of kids you can always count on. They're the ones who are serious about their walk with Christ, and want to be discipled. The other kids don't realize they rely on the core group, but they do. Your core group makes the program work, because they get behind the program. They become the peers of your group's peer pressure. Clyde understood all this. I didn't even know the words.

On the other hand, I had doubts about some of the ways Clyde wanted to implement his ideas on building a core group. His role playing game, a kind of Christianized Dungeons and Dragons, made me nervous. We gave it a try for a while. It had strengths, requiring thoughtful interaction on scripture and morality, and Bible memorization. I could never get the hang of the game. At one point, we were "attacked by a dragon," so I quoted a passage that was supposed to help in time of need. "You wasted that passage on a dragon?" He was astounded that I was so frivolous. Silly me, I thought dragons were bad. He told me dragons just chased you around and hurt you some, but usually didn't kill you. I liked the part about learning the Bible, but there was too much emphasis on techniques, not enough on real life.

Another game technique I couldn't get the hang of was speculating out loud. Something or other would happen in the game, and I would think to myself, "Oh, I see what's going on." It would be leading toward some spiritual truth or application. A couple of minutes later, one of the other players would say "Oh, I see what's going on! It's leading toward this spiritual truth or application!" Clyde would respond, "Good observation! For being the first to recognize this, you gain this cool new ability to turn your enemy's weapons into blue jello. I'm surprised you didn't catch onto that, Ferd." No matter how many times this happened, I never learned to think out loud. Considering what I thought sometimes, it might be good I kept my thoughts to myself.

I gave it a legitimate try, but I just couldn't get behind this as a discipleship tool. Since I was too slow on the uptake for Clyde, in his frustration, and unknown to me, he started to go ahead without me. We developed disagreements over materials and such, but we still managed to maintain our working partnership. Our final disagreement came when we couldn't agree on whether he should leave his wife, and we parted ways.

There were two brothers who tried to help me at different times. I wish I had paid better attention to them, because either one of them would have done a better job than two of me. They were about my age, had grown up in a solid Christian home, and had a huge edge on me—they had actually been in a Youth Group once!

One of them, Duane, started talking to me one day about Christian Camping. I was not even vaguely interested. In my opinion, Christian camping was nothing but an expensive play time in Jesus' name. My opinion was totally ignorant, but I don't let minor details like knowledge get in my way.

I declared camping expensive and unprofitable, and not worth the effort it would take to try to get any of my economically challenged kids to go. I knew I was right, too, because I went to camp when I was 10. The fact it wasn't a Christian camp didn't make any difference, either. I was an expert. Because I was so expert, I didn't listen to Duane, the helpful Christian who had no reason to offer help, other than his desire to serve Christ, help me do a good job, and benefit the kids.

During my last summer at First Big, somebody pulled a fast one on me, and sponsored a couple of bus ministry kids to camp without consulting me. Since some of "my" kids were going, I decided to go as a counselor (for someone who didn't know enough to make decisions, I sure decided a lot of things), just to prove my point about Christian camping, and further establish my credentials as an expert.

After only a few hours, I recognized—not decided—that Christian camp was somewhat better than some ignoramus had led me to believe. We should have more of our kids here! If I'd started doing this sooner, some of my older kids could have been here as workers! How come no one ever told me about this? Sorry, Duane. You tried.

Today I am a huge fan of Christian camps. Used properly, they are the among most powerful evangelism and discipleship tools available for young people.

Duane had better luck with me when we talked about a retreat. It helped that his parents had a lake cabin. Even I thought this was a good idea. Duane planned the activities, Sweetie handled the meals, I did the lessons. I hadn't learned yet to trust other speakers. I had this idea I had to do it all, or I wasn't earning my money. I had a hard time letting Duane plan the activities!

Since he grew up spending summers on this lake, Duane knew exactly what we should do. We walked about two miles around the end of the lake to a rock he called "The Plunge" directly across from the cabin. The rock loomed about 40 feet above the water. Anyone who jumped off the rock got a boat ride back. Anyone who would not jump had to walk back. This had become the basis of our retreat theme: "Plunge Into Jesus." Good evangelism theme, good "no turning back" theme, if you can get the kids to jump. But that's another story. For a retreat, it was a great advance.

Duane's brother Don was better with small group things, and came to me with ideas from time to time. I'd like to say my approval was based on ministry value, looking for truly teachable opportunities, but I have to be honest—I looked for fun. One time Don suggested rock-climbing. To check it out, we took Jose, always good for a challenge, and went to a local place popular for rock-climbing.

I wore jeans and a T-shirt. Don brought all sorts of gear. When I was a boy, if we wanted to get to the top of a rock, we climbed it without first putting on about 15 pounds of safety equipment and ropes. I'm such a dinosaur. Everyone knows that today's rocks require expensive stuff.

Jose and Don were wearing Jeans and sleeveless T-shirts.

At the bottom of a rock, Don was describing the proper way to climb and what gear to use, when some guy sauntered by us and just climbed the rock.

"Why can't we do like him?" I asked.

"Because he's really good, and you've never done this before." Well, I'd never done it with gear before. When I was a boy, my brother, cousins and I had "Club Rock." If you could climb to the top, you were in the club. If you couldn't, we laughed at you as you fell.

When they weren't looking, I tore my sleeves off. I noticed their sideways glances of admiration. A couple of rock climbers walked by who had taken the collars off their T-shirts.

Loaded down with all the proper gear, and practicing proper techniques, it was pretty difficult to climb that rock. We took turns climbing up and down these not so difficult looking rocks, talking about how we'd do something difficult once we finally got this mastered.

Once, when the two of them came down from the rock, they tried not to look enviously at my T-shirt without a collar.

We went to the top of a cliff and rappelled down. Now, that was something we never did at Club Rock. You stand on the top of a cliff, hanging onto a rope, with all sorts of weird gear hung all over you. Then you lean backwards to a 90 degree angle, so you are essentially standing up in a laying down position. Then you jump straight up, but since you're standing lying down, jumping straight up takes you straight out. What a blast! I could have done it all day, but Don seemed to think we were just evaluating it for Youth Group purposes. We never did this as a group, because I didn't have the patience to wait my turn. Besides, rock climbing is hard on your wardrobe.

Mr. Lodge, my most faithful co-worker aside from Sweetie, was fun and easygoing, and had a lot of good ideas. We also had a natural tie—He and his wife hosted the Bible study where I got saved! He never came in and tried to run the show, but understood very well how to come alongside and guide a youth director who didn't know he was ignorant.

He helped on retreats, various events, and our Mission Trip, and kept the bus running. He was an expert at working behind the scenes, which was important to me, since I thought my job required me to be up front and in control.

I guess the last co-workers I should write about are the kids themselves. They were very good at evaluating some of the different things that we tried. Sometimes we would involve them up front in the planning, asking them for their opinions. "Come on," I would say. "Don't be afraid of hurting my feelings. I know it's difficult to share your honest feelings with someone you respect and admire, and you may find it near traumatic if you feel the need to disagree with me in…"

"That's okay Ferd," Lawrence would finally interject, "It's a stupid idea and if you do it no one will show up."

Which is why we would sometimes involve them in the planning. Traumatic as it is to have one of your youth group members tell you your idea is stupid, it's worse to plan an event and have no one show up. Although, not showing up is one of the more effective ways teens express their opinions on an event.

They also had this unusual practice of holding one hand to their forehead and pretending to laugh while bending over from the waist. I never understood exactly what they were trying to communicate, but it usually seemed to translate something like: "I'm sorry, but I'm busy that day and won't be able to go."

O Christmas Tree

You are aware, I hope, how difficult it is to do things that "Anyone can do." In truth, there are very few things anyone can do, but one of them, apparently, is to say "Anyone can do it." I know from personal experience anyone cannot do it. Which just goes to prove anyone can be wrong.

In my youth group experience, those "anyone" kinds of things were: "Anyone can drive a bus," "Anyone can take care of a boiler," and "Anyone can get a Christmas tree." It's easy to explain the "Anyone cans." Those who can, can, and since they can, they think anyone can. The guy who drives a bus thinks it's no big deal to drive a bus. The guy who understood the boiler could never understand that, no, I didn't understand the boiler. The Christmas tree…

"Wait," You might say, "Anyone *can* get a Christmas tree." "Oh my child," I respond. "You are young and inexperienced. Have a seat, and I will explain to you the complexity of the simple." Taking care of a boiler or driving a bus, these are technical things. You either can do them or you can't. Their complexity makes this fact simple. Getting a tree is entirely different. The simplicity makes doing it right very difficult. Anyone can do it, but Everyone has a different idea of how it should be done. Anyone has to be able to please Everyone, which No One can do. Being ignorant of all this, when They suggested the youth group get this year's Sanctuary tree, saying "Anyone can do it," I accepted.

Being young and foolish, I thought that "anyone can do it" meant anyone can do it any way he'd like. I took this as an opportunity to do something really special. First Big had a huge sanctuary. Including the balcony, it could seat 1,000 people, though I never saw that many people there. This facility just cried out for a super jumbo economy-sized tree, but every year we saw another house size tree, dwarfed like a star in space. This had to change. It was time for First Big's first big "Youth Group Tree."

Someone in the group had someone in his family with land where we could go chop down any tree we wanted. I called the group together one December Saturday. We loaded on the bus, drove there with an ax, a handsaw, and rope. Several trees stood before us that less inspired people might have quickly accepted. In fact, several less inspired people kept telling me, "Ferd, this is a nice tree, can we go now?"

"No." I kept telling everyone. "Remember how big the sanctuary is."

Finally I saw the tree of my dreams. "It's too big!" Everyone protested. "You'll never get it in the bus!" So inexperienced they were. They didn't understand that with a little pressure anyone could bend the branches and slide it in the back door. It's a good thing so many kids came to help, because it took three of us taking turns to cut it down. Then it took all of us to haul it to the bus. Wood can be very heavy.

I am the 1996 Camp Chuchiwawa Chubby Bunny champion, and I know how to compress things. But even with my expertise, after a half hour of trying to force that larger-than-I-thought-it-was-tree into that smaller-than-I-thought-it-was-bus-door, I had to make a confession. "Guys, anyone can see this tree won't go in the bus." In fact, that tree wouldn't even go on top of the bus; at least not without whatever kind of equipment they used to put King Kong in the oil tanker. So we loaded a few smaller trees for home use and left our prize, secure in the knowledge that someone knew someone who knew how to get his hands on a truck with a hoist, and would get the tree to church.

Sure enough, the Tree materialized down at Big First that afternoon. Some joker had attached a very real looking "Wide Load" sign to it. Now all we had to do was get it in the front doors, down the hall, make a right turn through the sanctuary doors, and down the aisle. After that, it was as simple as standing it up, and how hard can that be? Anyone could do it.

The damage to all those doors was remarkably slight, and besides, the only witnesses would have implicated themselves in making accusation, so everyone was safe. Cleanup on the carpet wasn't too bad either. You just have to do those things quickly, while it's fresh. All the snow melting off the tree kept the carpet wet, too, and that helped.

Standing the tree up was an interesting process, and a photo might have resembled the flag-raising Marines of Iwo Jima. A couple of people put a foot to the trunk to brace the tree, and pulled. Four or five were on the other side, pushing and lifting. But the real key was the group on the balcony with the ropes. Pull from the top, push from the bottom, don't let the base slip, everyone works together a little, and voila! (that's French for "Wha-la!") It's up! Forget the Iwo Jima photo, we should have videotaped the whole process and made some real money!

The ropes were a good idea, too, and we decided to leave them there. It wouldn't do to have the tree fall over to Emphasize one of Pastor K's points. I have this mental image of him getting excited and pounding the pulpit. Then we hear the beginnings of a creak. A crack. A groan. Everyone looks in horror as the tree from the black lagoon topples, wiping out Pastor K. and the first three rows. Luckily, the first three rows were always empty. In fact, until that tree left, the whole south side of the sanctuary was empty. If you think it couldn't have fallen, that's what the people of Jericho thought when the Israelites blew their trumpets. At least the people at First Big had the good sense to be afraid. Of course, the tree didn't fall because of that rope, which just goes to prove that I'm smarter than those people at Jericho.

Having delivered the tree, the youth group was off the hook. You know, the hook, like the hook on a Christmas ornament, the one I didn't manage to avoid. That evening the Young Adults held a decorating party (this was a long time ago, when Sweetie and I were young adults). To this point I'd never given much thought to how anyone decorated those huge trees they have in New York and Washington DC. Someone should have thought this through. Having no cranes, scaffolding, or abominable snowmen, we made do with what we had. The lower part we decorated in the old fashioned way. We had to develop a whole new system for the other eighty percent. We liked our system so much we even gave it a name: "Throwing." I like to think it gave things a nice random effect.

I went to sleep that night quite confident this tree would impress people. I didn't even consider that high speed collisions also make an impression. In fact, looking at the expression on everyone's face, it's a very similar impression.

Believe it or not, the following year someone tagged the youth group to get the church tree again, which proves that high as my IQ is, someone at First Big was every bit my intellectual equal. I had learned my lesson, though, not everyone appreciates creative expression, and set my sights on a smaller tree.

On this second attempt, I took three of the guys to a national forest in pursuit of the perfect tree. Having never tree-hunted this way before, I thought it would be relatively simple. We'd drive to the woods and within minutes find four ideal trees out of the tens of thousands of beautiful specimens available. I didn't know we'd get there and find there was better parking at the mall. I think we picked the one precise moment of history when there were more people there than at any other time, because if it was always that busy, the forest would be called "Mount Baldy."

Undeterred, we plunged a little deeper into the forest than everyone else, always looking for the perfect tree. There are very few perfect trees. Trees in nature tend to grow in clumps, and don't fill out. It would be really nice to thin out a clump of scrawny trees so one could fill out nicely; but it's a little late to start when you're there with your ax. Besides, we each had a permit for one tree only, and forest rangers are not known for leniency. We just kept hiking further and further, eventually finding our four trees—three for ourselves, one for church. Now we just needed to get them home.

Since there was snow on the ground, it wouldn't have been hard to trace our steps back to the car, but that's much too tedious. Since we could hear cars on the highway, surely it would be quicker to follow our ears to the highway, take a left, and carry our trees to the car without having to maneuver them through the woods. Our ears failed to detect we would arrive at the top of a cutting, 20 or 30 feet above the highway.

Minor difficulty. Interesting challenge. Possible thrill. People pay money for rides like this! First we slid a tree down. It seemed to survive the trip intact, so we decided it must be safe. As the Responsible Youth Group Leader, I was the first human down (at least, that's the story I'll stick to, but I can't guarantee it—too many blows to the head). At any rate, it was kind of fun. You just sit in the snow, find yourself leaning forward at this incredible angle, and go! Soon there were four intact trees and three intact people down by the highway, and one hesitant soul at top of the cutting, also intact. Perhaps if he'd stayed at the top he'd have stayed intact. But you never know what might have been.

I never saw anyone slide downhill crooked before! Four trees went straight downhill. Three guys went straight downhill. Everyone had already proven that anyone could do it! But someone went down at this cockeyed angle, and it wasn't even me! I don't know if that last guy was weighted differently than the rest of us or what, but there was only one stick in the ground anywhere near us, and that one stick held some kind of powerful attraction for him. We yelled, he squirmed, wiggled, rolled, and did everything possible, but somehow that stick drew him. Nothing broke, and he avoided having to haul a tree back to the car.

Other than that, the tree for the church was a big, can I say…'hit'? Everyone liked it.

The Hats You Wear

One of the things you realize before you've been in the ministry very long is that you haven't taken a job, you've taken several. Sometimes this is called 'wearing several hats.' In my case, this sometimes meant 'wearing several costumes.' I think this began for me the year I became—Dada da Duh: Rainbow Man!

Rainbow Man was the theme character for VBS one year. I don't remember many particulars about being Rainbow Man, but we superhero types do so many things, it's hard to remember details. We're also modest. I wore a funny cardboard hat, and a cape that in its other identity posed as a common everyday child's bedroom curtain. No one ever suspected.

If I had to guess, I'd say that was the year our VBS theme was "God Keeps His Promises," with the rainbow representing promise keeping. Years later, when Promise Keepers came out, I found myself hesitant to accept the idea because of the name. It had been ground into my thinking that man makes promises, but God keeps promises, which really is a sobering thought. Still, an organization called "Promise Attempters" would never get off the ground, so I finally lightened up. Besides, Promise Keepers doesn't make you wear a funny hat and cape.

The danger of being Rainbow Man was too subtle for me to realize until it was too late. The damage done, a precedent set. Everyone now knew Ferd would put on funny clothes and do foolish things. When you think about it, that's really not such a stretch. I still put on a suit and tie, and what clothing is possibly more foolish than that? At least a funny hat and cape won't strangle you.

I wore another hat, much simpler, and far more flattering. We took one of those political white Styrofoam hats with a red, white, and blue paper hatband, painted it black, and put "the Boss" on it in white. I kind of liked being "The Boss." The Boss doesn't even teach a class, but wanders from room to room, peeking in and causing trouble. He speaks to large groups, and is important. He spends an inordinate amount of time in the kitchen doing quality control, because a good boss doesn't make his crew eat anything he wouldn't eat himself. (And he tells Lawrence to sneak more sugar into the Kool-Aid because the Cookie Lady thinks it's healthier to cut it in half, and it tastes terrible that way.)

He also spends a fair amount of time with his feet up on his desk, being important.

One of the duties of The Boss is discipline. This is a very important job when you're running a bus ministry, because some of these kids are slightly unclear on behavior rules: things like, 'don't swear at the teachers,' and 'no knives and guns.' We developed an effective yet non-violent technique I still use (you can't use Youth Group Discipline, children are too frail). I take the child into my office, sit him in a chair, and ignore him for about five minutes. For a ten year old, five minutes is something just shy of eternity. He gets no toys, no books, and can't talk or leave the chair. Then, looking up from the book you'd been wanting to read anyway, you notice him, and say, "If I let you go back, will you do it again?" At this point some kids actually volunteer to do more time, but most submit. Getting his agreement, you escort him back, make him apologize, and life is good.

Just the sight of The Hat in the hallway calms a room, and even the kids who might cause trouble the rest of the time don't when you're around. Being The Boss was pretty cool. Naturally, it had it's sneaky down side.

Every VBS needs promotions. Memory verse contests, Missionary projects, Who can bring the most friends, and so on.

"What can we do for the child who brings the most friends?" I asked.

"I know, they get to hit someone in the face with a pie!"

"Great idea! How about the secretary!" I would have liked to hit the secretary with a pie.

"No, Ferd, it's got to be you!" Lawrence piped up. Of course the secretary agreed pretty quickly, and almost before the suggestion was made, the whole planning group (minus one) was in favor.

If I'm The Boss, how come this decision was made for me and not by me? Dazed and trying to figure this out, I missed the vote. My one vote might not have made any difference, but at least it wouldn't have been unanimous.

I made the sacrifice. The kids knew me. They liked me. At least, they liked the idea of hitting me in the face with a pie. The noise they made on Monday when this was announced foretold the biggest Bible School we'd ever run. This had to be the best idea we'd ever come up with, and we'd have to do this every year!

On Tuesday, they made a lot of noise again, but no one had brought any friends. On Wednesday, more noise, but no more friends. Maybe a couple of kids brought a friend, but this wasn't what I'd bargained for. Thursday: as much noise as if they were all bringing friends like crazy and the contest was close. Sure it was close; like two zeros on a scoreboard is close.

Friday, driving the bus, we got to the Dixon's house, and little Jessie Dixon had two friends with her. She crowed, knowing that two friends on the last day won the contest for her. I had a hard time being as thrilled as she was. Not only was she going to win by bringing only two friends for only one day, but I was provided the ride! I managed to conceal my excitement.

I didn't get the pie in the face on Friday morning during VBS, but Friday evening, with a church full of parents. It turned out that while this hadn't developed into a great draw for Bible School, it was a great draw for the closing program. It's hard to get parents to come out for a Friday evening closing, but these kids were not going to be denied. Mom and dad either brought them to church, or suffered the consequences. It was easily the best attended closing program we'd ever done. The kids quoted their verses, sang their songs, and showed off their crafts. Pastor Kahuna gave an evangelistic message that hopefully hit some hearts.

Soon, there were only two things left to do, and one of them was to go downstairs for dessert after the other one was complete. So there we were, little Jessie Dixon and a great big pie, with The Boss on his knees so she could reach.

I wasn't too worried. Little Jessie Dixon was, after all, little. She might miss me entirely! Yeah, right. Did you know you can drown on whipped cream? I don't know anyone who's actually done it, but I know someone who thought he might be the first.

Her dad must have coached her, because the way she smashed that pie would make a circus clown proud. I know his motivation: "Drag me out to a VBS program on Friday evening, you'd better make it worth my time!" She made it worth his time.

She had the technique down so that after solidly smashing my face with the pie, she continued pushing the plate in an upward motion. In pie-tossing circles, that is called the "follow through." It has the double effect of not only smearing the cream completely over your face, but of shoving it about a foot and a half up your nostrils, so far it seeps out your ears. If I ever get hit in the face with a pie again, I plan to take a timely deep breath first.

I learned something new about First Big that day—those people are extremely low on compassion! The church went wild, Jessie was a hero, and we all went downstairs for dessert. Everyone else ate heartily, but I'd already had my fill.

My most elaborate outfit ever was the year I played Psalty the Singing Songbook (a real imaginary character). I have a hard time figuring out what happened—Someone Else wanted to do the play, Someone Else thought I should do the part, Someone Else thought it wouldn't be hard to make the costume, yet

Someone Else did nothing but think of what others should do. Psalty the Singing Sucker might have been more appropriate.

I start with a refrigerator box, which is the only box big enough and heavy enough to do the job. I cut, folded, stapled and mutilated until I had a rough book shape, and then covered it with blue felt. Once I'd done all this real work (or at least claim I did it, even though Sweetie did it while I gave helpful advice), Someone Else gladly did a few artistic things to it to make it look more like a songbook. A bit of Styrofoam with lines passed for pages. The hardest part of the whole costume was rigging a harness that let me stick my face out the hole while keeping the book upright and facing the right direction.

Again, I don't remember the actual program. Fortunately, Sweetie had painted my face blue (which ended up a slight purple because we didn't compensate for the red my embarrassment added), and gave me a measure of anonymity. The good costume helped make up for my bad singing and acting, and the kids did great on their part of the play.

After the program, we stashed Psalty down in the church basement, which was fortunately large. It wouldn't be long 'til we pulled him out to do another Psalty play, because you don't go to all the trouble of making a costume like that and only use it once, right? If you ever go through the work of making a costume like that, at least do yourself the service of pretending it will be used more than once. That way you might believe it's worth the effort. Bunny Dixon asked one year if she could borrow it for a costume party. I said yes, it was destroyed, and it never again took up half our storage.

One year, I was an old man in the Christmas play. Someone had one of those full face masks for me to wear, and when I put it on, I became a pretty convincing little old man. Pastor Kahuna and I set up a promotional, where I would "go to church" as the old man, and share during announcements.

I got hold of a patterned heavy winter coat—an old man coat—and walked into church, moving slow, and a little stooped. One of the ushers tried to help me to a seat, but I didn't want anyone to get too close, and I knew exactly where I wanted to sit. I shrugged him off like a crotchety old man, and shuffled down front.

I felt everyone staring at me, and wished I could read their minds. Either it was "Who is that elderly man?" Or "What is that stupid Ferd up to now? Does he think he's fooling anyone?" Considering the average age in the congregation, some of the women might even have been wondering if I was single!

On cue, Pastor Kahuna started to announce the Christmas program. I interrupted. My chest was so tight with nerves I could hardly speak with the volume I needed, but that might have helped the effect. I complained in a loud voice about how people abuse and misuse Christmas, how it's been commercialized and trivialized, all the while shuffling toward the podium. Pastor K. gracefully allowed the old gentleman to take his place at the podium, and I finally got to look at the congregation that had been looking at me all this time. Did they know? Were they wondering how long they had to put up with Ferd's antics? Did I have any dates lined up?

If I have any ability to read faces, they were horrified. "What is going on here?" "Why is Pastor Kahuna letting this old geezer take charge of the service?" "I don't care if this guy is single!" Finally, it was time to take the mask off and announce the play. I peeled it off and looked at their faces, and it was clear I had pulled it off. The shock and laughter when they realized who I was could not be denied.

After the service, one of the men came up to me and said "You did a good job, but I knew it was you all the time. I told him thanks for not telling, but my thoughts were "Who do you think you're kidding, you old goat." Of course, I flatter myself. He was probably thinking "Who did you think you were kidding, you young punk?"

Over the years I've worn cowboy hats, sombreros, kafia (the towel-like things they wear in the Middle east), Chinese Coolie hats, and baseball caps of all types. My favorite bears my name: Grumpy. I've worn long wigs and bald wigs and a pink wig. I've been Old Testament characters, New Testament characters, and Humpty Dumpty. "What do you do for a living?" You ask, "Are you an actor?"

"No, I d serious work. I'm a Pastor!"

Heavy Metal Christians

Have you ever wondered if David made any money singing Psalms? Maybe someday an archaeologist will come across a 3,000 year old promotional poster that reads "Coming to Hebron...DAVID AND THE MIGHTY MEN! Singing their new hit, Psalm 23! Opening for the concert, that rising new group, Trees Of The Field!" Until that day, I'll continue to believe David's music was between him and the Lord, and continue to wonder how many people today would feel so "called" to Christian music if there weren't money to be made.

My own experience with Christian concerts, aside from going to them, is somewhat less than big-time. There's the one I avoided, and the one I didn't. The two cover the entire spectrum of what can be called music. I managed to duck the Opera Guy, and got hit head on by Heavy Metal.

The Opera Guy, I'm sure was good, though I'll never really know. Pastor Kahuna lined him up for a Sunday evening because he knew the whole church would be marvelously blessed. I immediately and quietly arranged for the Youth Group to visit another church that evening with a contemporary group performing. I said nothing about my plans to anyone but the Youth Group for as long as I could.

Finally, Pastor K. said something like: "I bet the kids are really looking forward to having their musical horizons expanded with Opera Guy this Sunday, Huh?"

I put on my most sincerely shocked look. "Oh no! Is that this Sunday? I already committed to taking the kids to hear Bread & Whine across town!" Somehow, I convinced him that this was okay, and we didn't have to stay for Opera Guy. Maybe a better way to say it is, I didn't have to stay for Opera Guy. The kids would have stayed home that night.

I know, my whole technique sounds less than saintly. I can think of all sorts of ways to defend it, things like: "Hey, it worked, didn't it," and so on. You can't really defend a lie, so I'm not saying I did right, I'm just saying what I did.

Bread & Whine, by the way, was a small drama and contemporary music group, a couple of the members went to Bible College with me. They weren't rich or famous, but they did what they did out of a sincere desire to minister in Christ's name.

The program was thoroughly enjoyable, until someone paged me for a phone call. It was Pastor Kahuna, wanting to know if I'd borrowed the sound system from church.

"No, I didn't. I think that might be a wrong thing to do." This turned out to be one of the three or four times the church was robbed during my time there. That ruined his concert for him, and mine for me, but the kids enjoyed the show. And it was still better than my other concert experience.

Since First Big was big and downtown, we sometimes got requests from interesting people for the facilities. One day Pastor K. got a visit from a group of young men who looked slightly out of place in a large, old church building. As if guys with long multi-directional and multi-colored hair, strange jewelry, ragged jeans and expensive leather look in place anywhere! He welcomed them into his office, and I prayed for him. If I'd known what they were there for, I'd have prayed harder.

After they left his office, he called me over. "Ferd, we're going to put on a Christian Concert. I want you to oversee it."

"Pastor K., you are the Senior Pastor, with experience and wisdom beyond the scope of my imagination, but I don't think this is a good idea."

"Ferd, Krash 4 Jesus and Bern 4 God are fine examples of godly young musicians. Hosting this concert will double the Youth Group and gain you respect in the eyes of your colleagues." I think it would also pay me back for skipping Opera Guy.

"Pastor K., you have far greater experience than me, and I have no right to question you, but are you sure? No one has ever been able to make out the lyrics of Krash or Bern, and we don't even know if there's anything Christian about them. Not one kid in the Youth Group likes either band. We'll probably have to cordon off the church or people will wander all over the place Then we have to get everything cleaned up before services in the morning."

"Ferd, it's good to hear you're already working out the details. You WILL enjoy doing this."

It's so good to know I'll enjoy something. I often found this kind of joy in my work. It was James who said "Consider it all joy, my brethren, when you encounter various trials." I suspect James was youth pastor before he was a martyr.

Since he was Pastor Kahuna, and I was Ferd, I did it. I met with band members, and we planned the thing. A third band, Bang 4 the Spirit joined the party, so we started publicizing the Krash, Bang, and Bern Concert.

The groups handled publicity, they would do all the set up and take down. I just had to be there. We planned to all pray and share the Lord's Supper together before the concert, which put me somewhat at ease. Anyone who prays and shares the Lord's Supper together before their concert must have their act together.

Everyone raced around the night of the concert. No one had his act together enough to find time to pray or share the Lord's Supper together. After all, it takes a lot of time to remove two rows of large, padded, bolted down pews, and to properly set up smoke machines, lights, speakers, and other band equipment. In fact, it's a good thing they took as much time as they did, or the pews might have been damaged even more.

The Board became aware of this concert I had arranged and gave me explicit instructions to protect the property. "Ferd, Pastor Kahuna told us about your concert. You'd better not let anything happen to our church." I managed to entice four Youth Group guys to come that evening. We strung ropes, hung No Admittance signs, and stationed ourselves strategically to prevent people from abusing the place, leaving ourselves room to run if we had to.

The bands Krashed, Banged, and Berned just fine. When people poured out of the Sanctuary during a break, I tried to mingle with some of the less scary looking, and they seemed satisfied. None of my group actually went in the Sanctuary during the concert. This was fine, since the music was more than loud enough after traveling through the walls. Fortunately, this prevented us from feeling compelled to try and stop the fight, because it was over before we knew about it. I guess it didn't last too long, and no one got hurt too badly. That kind of thing happens at Christian concerts where people wear chains. I didn't hear about it until I asked why that bloody guy was leaving.

The thing ended some time early Sunday morning, when the blurry hands on the blurry clock were near the blurry numbers. The kids and I did some clean-up, then I took them home, while the bands started to pack up their stuff. I swung back by the church to help the guys, see how they thought it went, and see if they wanted to pray and share the Lord's Supper together after the concert. I came in the door and just listened to them talk a little. They discussed how the evening went. They talked about musical technique. They compared who could hit the higher note. No one said anything about, oh…Jesus, or, say, ministry. I helped them put the pews back, then went home to get two or three hours of sleep so I'd be in good shape to drive the bus.

Sunday morning reactions: "Why is there this cloud hanging in the Sanctuary?" "What happened to this pew?" "Why is the front set up so differently?" "I can't find my microphone." "Is Ferd snoring?"

Monday morning reactions: "Ferd, things were left a mess after the concert."

"Yes, Pastor K. I noticed that myself."

"Well, let's chalk this one up to experience. But between you and me, Ferd, I don't think you should do another one of those here."

"You're very wise, Pastor K. I'll try to remember that."

My Favorite Games

There are these marvelous things out there called "Game Books." I know about them now, but it was news to me when I started. Actually, it wasn't news to me, but it would have been had anyone cared to tell me. As it was, I, Ferd the Clueless, with no grasp of games, tried to lead Youth Group. Even I knew we needed them.

One of the kids knew this game called "Sardines." Just in case you're such a novice you don't know Sardines, it's pretty simple—Hide and Seek played backwards. One person hides in the dark building, in a place with enough room for (theoretically) everyone to fit. After a set amount of time, everyone starts searching for the hider, and when you find him, you join him. The last person to find him is the loser. Hiding places are limited by your imagination.

Taking advantage of the dark, one of my most successful ploys was to sit down in the middle of a room. Searchers would enter a room, grope around the walls, feel all around tables and chairs, then leave. No one ever looks for someone hiding in the open.

First Big was a quarter of a city block around, and three stories tall, with an abundance of assorted crawl spaces, nooks, and crannies. Whoever first dreamt up Sardines had this building in mind. I had to rule some places off limits: the bell tower (which had to be reached by ladder), the boiler room, the crawl space next to the boiler room, the sanctuary, and…the baptistry.

For some reason, the baptistry called to the kids. "Come to me, I'll hide you." I could never understand this. It didn't call to them to be baptized. Only two of the kids ever were baptized in it, but they all wanted to hide there. Instead of calling it "the baptismal" we should have called it "the hiding place." My constant nagging didn't affect them, and I had to patrol the area, chasing them away.

One day, when the siren song hit the kids pretty solidly, I missed it. Several of them sneaked in before I figured it out, scoped it out, and heard them giggling. My first instinct almost had me storm in yelling and lecturing, but inspiration hit. Actually, it didn't hit me, I hit it. Inspiration looks a lot like a shin high faucet handle. You know, the kind of handle on one side of the wall to control the faucet on the other side of the wall. This was when I learned how much fun it is to turn giggles into screams. It's almost natural sounding, too. It goes something like: "Ha ha HAAAAAAAAAA!" My turn to giggle. Why should the kids have all the fun?

I also learned that day that wet kids don't want to play Sardines, so we had to move on to another game. But the call of the baptismal was broken, and it was never again an attractive hiding place.

Caveman Football always appealed to my more primitive side. You must carefully consider many factors when deciding to play Caveman Football, things like: Do you allow some to watch from the sidelines, are there any hard objects around, and is everyone properly insured? I'm not sure I recommend this game, but I like it.

Caveman Football is like football, only you don't use a football. You just tackle people. One person stands in the middle of a field. A park is ideal. A large lawn will do, I've played in rough ground, but paid the price. The rest of the players line up at one end of the field, and at a given signal they try to reach the other end without getting taken down. Anyone who gets tackled by the 'Middleman' stays in the middle, now transformed from a "tacklee" into a "tackler." The last untackled person becomes the next middleman.

The first time I ever played this, it was strictly "guys only," but what can I say? Girls like to play this game! Most guys instinctively know to be a little gentler with girls, though I once saw a streak-of-lightning-fast high school senior guy plow over this unsuspecting-small-Junior-High-girl exactly the way the Coyote has always wanted to unleash on the Roadrunner. I was truly shocked when she got up on her own power, a little dazed, but still wanting to play. The boy and I had a short one-sided conversation, and I made it a policy you save the big hits for someone big enough to take it.

Speaking of big hits, I personally loved this game. Being a small person (though I'm now big where it really counts—in the middle), I've always tended to suffer from "Little Big Man's Syndrome." You know—the little guy who acts big. My favorite place to live this out in my growing up years was football. I wasn't athletic enough to throw the ball, or fast enough to run the ball, or big enough to block anybody. Fortunately, I was dumb enough to throw my body in front of large moving objects. I loved tackling. I didn't need physics to understand the relationship between speed, mass, and impact, because I knew from experience. Anybody, of any bulk, moving at any speed, if he had the ball, I found a way to hit him and take him down. More than once they had to find my remains somewhere under some larger body, put me on my feet, and point me in the right direction. I was in heaven, I'd taken him down.

Still, I never played organized football. I was way too small. I stood five foot zero when I entered a large high school. By the time I got to my impressive full size of 5'7" and 125 pounds, like when I graduated, it was a little too late to catch up. But a group of us played on Saturday afternoons, and we played until too many of us were too injured to continue. Blood, limps, mild concussions, and things like that. One guy broke his nose once, but continued playing. One Saturday, some of the 'real' football players joined us, and we showed them what it's like to play without padding. I remember it with a smile, because they had nothing on us.

All this to say, Caveman Football put me right in my element.

One day, in a move I thought was funny, we put a small 7th grade boy in the middle to start the game. There was only one problem—he couldn't tackle anyone. A few years later he became a starting high school linebacker and I didn't want to play with him anymore, but at this particular time, he wasn't doing so well. We all ran by, and he jumped on someone who carried him past the line. He trotted back to the middle and tried again, with the same success. His personal standards kept him from tackling the girls, and he couldn't get the guys. After about four passes, I decided I had to do something about it, so when we said "Go", I ran up to him, he jumped on me, and I fell down.

Now in the middle, I prepared to have some fun. I immediately set my sights on 200 pounds of 6'3" Bubba. Bubba saw me coming, but didn't seem concerned, which is just too bad. That rock David threw wasn't big, either, but when it hit Goliath, he went down, and that's just what happened to Bubba. Still on the ground, I gloried in my victory when itty bitty Jr. High Susie came skipping my way. I figured if she was going to make it that easy, I might as well get two for one, and grabbed for her ankle.

It's kind of embarrassing. I lay flat on the ground, and did this little forward flop when I tried to grab her ankle. I just kind of lurched forward and grabbed. But Susie got away because I let go of her ankle when my rib cracked.

Proverbs 16:18 says "Pride goeth before destruction, and a haughty spirit before a fall." In my case, the order was a little mixed: First came the fall, then came the haughty spirit, then came destruction. You know you're special when God changes the order just for you.

Some people think the only games you play at church should be "Spiritual Games." Noncompetitive games where people are sincere and kind, where they learn things about themselves and others, with no winners and losers. The only thing I ever learned from those games is those people never worked with Youth

Group. Give me a game with action, and I don't care who loses, so long as I have a chance to win. Most kids feel the same way.

We once played a game that called for kids to dress up in army clothing. A father called and bawled me out, because Christianity has no place for such military connections. "We're supposed to be peaceful and nice." I thought about telling him about Joshua, or the armor of the Lord, but instead I just listened and said "Yes sir" and "No sir" at the proper times. The funny thing is, that was one of our more Christian-themed games. Based on the persecuted church, the kids were to sneak past soldiers to get to a covert Bible study.

Admittedly, most of our games were not "Christian themed." Take "Assassins," for example. While it's possible to tie a Christian theme to the military, it's hard to stretch things enough to justify murder. I didn't care. It sounded like fun, so we played Assassins.

I discovered this game in the Spring of my senior year, just before finals. I had a burning desire to play, but I wasn't sure it would fly. I needed a place to try it out before I played it with the kids, and I found just the place—Bible College! I figured this would not fly with the administration, so I didn't ask. Soon an anonymously posted note appeared in the snack room, with a brief description of the rules, and a sign up sheet. I expected too small a response for it work, but I think about half the student body signed up.

I don't know what people expect to find on a Bible college campus during finals week, but it probably doesn't include students racing down the halls with dart guns, hiding behind doors, or building barricades with tables in the snack room! Not only did all that happen that week, but even a couple of the profs joined in! One of them broke a rule by using a multiple-shot gun. But you don't bother Hebrew scholars over minor details like that. Besides, the game relied more on stealth than firepower.

To play Assassin, you put everyone's name on a sheet of paper. Each player draws a name, waits for an appointed starting time, then seeks to 'kill' the person whose name they drew. If you manage to assassinate your victim, then you take the name he has, and go after that person. There are no safe people, places, or times (putting it that way, maybe this *is* good ministry training!). Special arrangements need to be made for when someone gets his own name, which is bound to happen more and more as the game proceeds. A referee will be needed to call a truce, redistribute names among the survivors, and then begin 'Round Two.'

I could not both direct the game and protect my anonymity, and while I appeared to have fun (in spite of dying on day two, killed by a traitor I once thought of as a friend), on the inside I waited to be called on the carpet. I envisioned the scene repeatedly: Me, standing in front of a big desk, the school president, dean, chairman, and various board members there to make sure I know just how serious this was. I'm being expelled, won't graduate, and will get fired from the church. They're even checking with God to see if my salvation can be made probationary, and so on.

But the rebuke never came. Instead, an unofficial response filtered down to me from the dean of women: "Thank you. Everyone was under a lot of stress. This is just what they needed." I guess it's true God moves in mysterious ways. Sometimes He can even use Assassins.

A big hit on campus, when I took the game to Youth Group, it fizzled. Maybe even though God can use Assassins, He doesn't want to overdo it.

The Walkathon

Sweetie had a good idea one day: "Let's take the kids on the Walkathon!" March of Dimes held a 20 mile walkathon in our town every year. I had even gone once, when I was in high school myself (it impressed the babes). This idea had everything—Good cause, group-building, and a built-in lesson theme, by the time you're done, everyone would be ready for a nice footwashing. And more than that, since Sweetie came up with the idea, she had to help plan it, which means things would actually be organized! Someday I'm going to learn that trick.

We would have the kids spend the night, so we wouldn't have to race around early trying to gather everyone. We could also be sure everyone ate well before walking 20 miles. I would drop everyone off at the starting point, park the bus at First Big, about half a mile away, and walk back in time to start. After the trek, I'd walk back to the bus, and return to shuttle everyone to the church for a meal and footwashing. This meant an extra half mile for me both before and after the 20, but when you're going that far, what's one more mile? Piece of cake!

We gathered all our walkers at our house in time for dinner the night before, and experienced another of our many lessons on the volume of food teens can put away. We never seemed to learn that lesson, and I have a theory why. Trying to feed a youth group is like playing Russian Roulette, and losing. You never learn your lesson, because once you've blown your brains out, it's difficult to remember what happened.

In order to get everyone T-shirts, each walker had to raise at least $25.00. We challenged them all to each raise that much. Who wanted to walk 20 miles and not even get a T-shirt?

"How many of you raised your $25.00?" I asked. Most had fallen short, and some, between bites, just said "Huh?"

Sweetie is nothing if not determined. For example, when we got married she was determined to make a better man out of me, and she's still trying! Now she was determined each and every one of those kids was going to raise their $25.00. She grabbed the church directory, put them on the phone, told them who to call, and what to say. The typical conversation went something like this: "Hi, I'm (*Chomp*) <u>my name</u>, and I'd (*slurp*) like you to sponsor me for the (*belch*) March of…what march is this?" At this point Sweetie would grab the phone, quickly wipe off the mouthpiece with a Lysol soaked rag, and salvage the conversation. Invariably the person called made a hefty donation, I think to protect Sweetie from having to do this any more.

Early next morning we offered the kids a healthy breakfast. I even cooked, oatmeal being one of the three things I'm actually competent to cook (the other two are hamburgers and beans). An interesting phenomenon occurred. Have you ever wanted to see what happens when an irresistible force meets an immovable object? In this case, insatiable appetites met oatmeal. It may be a philosophical dilemma, but as far as I'm concerned you can throw philosophy out the window. Oatmeal wins every time. Well, I ate hearty, anyway. And it's a good thing—I was going to need some irresistible energy.

Things started well. I dropped the group off and Sweetie signed them in while I parked the bus and walked back. One half mile down, Forty-one half miles to go.

When the thing started, Cameron and Peter shot off running, shouting they'd see us at the end. I laughed and said something about the tortoise and the hare, but we truly didn't see them again until the end. To this day, they insist they ran the entire twenty miles. Part of me is thoroughly disgusted with their health and ability, but more of me is grateful. At least I didn't have to carry *them*.

At the halfway mark, they had a place set up for lunch. It was nice to sit a little and rest, but it's a big mistake to let a moving object stop if you want it to start moving again after a meal. Thus began the Ferd and Sweetie Shuttle Service.

Sweetie wore a sweater that day that never saw service again. It ought to be in the Sweater Hall of Fame for wear and tear beyond the call of duty. One girl grabbed handful of sweater on one side, another on the other side. Sweetie leaned forward, and started walking. At times she took just one and gave a piggy-back ride. I gave camel rides on my shoulders.

We did this the bulk of the second ten miles. I myself am not nice enough to do this. I myself am not even in the neighborhood of, or on speaking terms with, anyone nice enough to do this, but Sweetie was determined everyone was going to get one of those T-shirts, and her determination started rubbing off on me. Somewhere along the way, Walkathon officials came along in pickups offering to help those who felt the need to drop out. Some of the girls would have gladly hopped on board, but it meant no T-shirt, and if we had to coerce, carry, or drag them, they were going to get that shirt!

Somewhere along the way, it occurred to me that a man carrying teenagers on his shoulders during a walkathon might be just the kind of thing some TV or newspaper reporter might like to catch on film. Of course, being a naturally shy and humble person, I would try to avoid such a thing. But no matter how carefully I kept watch, I couldn't find any reporters to avoid. Too bad. I really would have liked people to realize how humble I was. Many still don't know.

Eventually, mercifully, we staggered across the line. Every last one. Peter and Cameron were there, full of life and joy, wondering what had taken us so long. Our girls who'd needed dragging were there, wondering about their ride to the church. I wondered about the idiot who volunteered me for that last half mile to the bus.

I have no memory what those shirts looked like. If I was to make this up, I'd have us all step out on the platform at church that Sunday, wearing those shirts, and say "Thank you for your support. With your help we raised XX Dollars for the March of Dimes." But we didn't. Or, if we did, I don't remember it. What I do remember is, I still had a half mile to walk. And everyone was going to wait unhappily until the bus came and picked them up, and "No, we won't walk with you, and could you please hurry, Ferd?"

Did I say Everyone was going to wait unhappily for the bus? I should have been so lucky. Instead, Cam and Peter came to get the bus with me. They ran, they laughed, they jumped, carefree and energetic and happy as can be. They're lucky I wasn't armed. I hate that happy stuff. I felt better once we got to the bus. Then if they got too joyful I could slam on the brakes and maybe throw them into something hard.

We got everyone back to the church basement for youth group heaven, meaning pop, pizza, and a washtub waiting for warm soapy water. Sweetie went into the kitchen and kids actually volunteered to help. I filled the tub and a line formed. The kids were as anxious to soothe their feet as they were to eat.

We blessed the food, blessed the day, blessed the lesson, and read John 13 about Jesus washing the disciples' feet. Then we let the kids eat. As they ate, Sweetie and I set two chairs next to the tub, got down on our knees, and started washing feet. I thought some of the kids would feel embarrassed about having someone wash their feet, but if anyone did, it didn't show. I think this was one of the most universally appreciated things we ever did.

I kept waiting for one of them to say, "Let me wash your feet, Ferd." But none of them did. Once everyone else was comfortable and shod, Sweetie and I washed each other's feet. It makes we wonder: in John 13, you never do see anyone washing Jesus' feet. Maybe John just didn't bother to write down that detail. Maybe they all jumped up and fought for the right as soon as Jesus sat down, and that degenerated into one of their arguments over who was greater. But maybe, His feet didn't get washed.

I can see Jesus say, "As I have done to you, so you ought to do to one another," then cast a casual glance at His still unwashed feet; look up, and catch a disciple's eye. A meaningful look, meaning: "If you guys aren't completely dense one of you will wash My feet!" Okay, I can't really see Jesus doing that, but I can see myself doing it! Still, I wonder if He ever shook His head and thought "Why do I bother? They never seem to get it."

On the other hand, eleven of those men turned the world upside down. There's still hope for my group.

The day was not over. They all needed rides home. The church basement needed cleaning. About two weary hours later we stumbled home to our own children who had been ignored since the night before. We had a lot to do to get ready for the next day, Sunday, another busy day.

I love Sweetie, but next time she has a good idea involving a walk, I'm going to walk the other way.

Tubing On The River

If you live in an area with a just-right river—not too deep, not too shallow, not too fast, not too slow, and not too polluted—you might try tubing down the river. First Big was located in a city with just such a river.

My friend Budge stopped by the house one innocent summer day, "Hey Ferd, lets go tubing on the river!" This translates: "I want to go tubing on the river, and my wife says I can't go alone." Also, when you go tubing, you need two vehicles, one to park at your "get in" point, and one at your "get out" point. Budge needed someone to help drive, and since unlike his other friends I had a valid drivers license, he favored me with the request.

We expected tubing to take all afternoon, and no way could I justify spending that much time just on myself. "Let me call one of the youth group kids, and we'll check it out for a group event." I got on the phone to Jose: "Hey Joe, let's go tubing on the river!" I could hear his thoughts: "This translates, 'I want to go tubing on the river and I need you to come and justify my time.'" Still, he said yes, and we planned to go that afternoon.

Back in those days, no one had yet figured out the advantage of spending $43.95 for a special tube that says "Water Tube." In our ignorance we went to the gas station and asked if they had any old tubes. They were glad to get rid of some. Today, because of safety concerns, they can't let you have old tubes that way. Instead, you go the sporting goods store and spend $43.95 for the tube you might fall off and drown.

We dropped one car off at our "get out" spot, then drove upriver about 7 miles, to a good starting point. We figured if the trip was too short, we could always go a second time.

It was great! We bounced through small shallow rapids where we could hang on and just ride through. Then we drifted through still pools, where we swam and dived and tried to drown each other (The only dangerous part of the trip, Budge being even less endowed with common sense than I am).

We played and swam, and laughed, and lazed in the sun and tanned. In fact, we developed one of the most amazing red tans you've ever seen. Personally, I didn't quickly notice the overzealous tan I developed, being distracted by friction burn. Laying your bare arms over hot black rubber, repeatedly hanging on or climbing on semi-smooth inflated surface is a sure recipe for pain. Picture a severe sunburn on your armpits. The insides of my arms burnt, the sides of my chest burnt, and my armpits burnt. It became much worse when those parts rubbed together. It's very hard to keep them from rubbing together. If more people understood this feeling, Jesus would have described hell as "where the burning on the inside of your armpit does not go away forever and ever." For the next week I shuffled around like a human scarecrow.

The trip also took three or four times as long as I thought it would. As the sun settled behind the trees, we wondered if we should get out and walk. Once it became really dark, we wondered if we'd recognize our 'get out' spot. It would be pretty hard to miss it, since a bridge crossed the river there, but when you're floating on a tube in a river in the dark, you begin to wonder.

I got home around 11:30, moaning, groaning, shuffling, scarecrowing, and smiling. I told Sweetie about it, and we decided it would make a great youth group activity.

Having learned a thing or two, we planned a shorter trip, told everyone to wear a sleeved T-shirt, and shoes they could take in the water. Everyone was supposed to come with their own tube, and a permission slip stating that if they drowned it was just too bad.

Sweetie and I, being experienced youth group leaders, gathered up as many extra tubes as we could. Good thing, too, since most of the kids showed up without tending to that minor detail. A couple of the tubes we brought were truly "emergency tubes," only to be used as a last resort. They must have come off mini-bikes, for the truly small-bunned youth group member. Sweetie and I took a couple of good tubes. At this point I figured if the kids aren't willing to get their own tubes, they just have to settle for what they can get. Some of the kids doubled up on some of the larger tubes, but Cindy and Melody had to single up on the ones that looked like economy size bagels.

Two workers for 25 teens at the time seemed like a terrific ratio to us, since it was often 1 to 30. Of course we had to be more responsible than usual, since water play presents the possibility of danger. As it turns out, the ratio was reversed: 12 1/2 kids were enough to take care of each leader. The only two in any danger were Sweetie and I.

We ran into the shallow rapids, about a foot of water running through a wide, 1/4 mile section of river. Mel and Cin on the bagel tubes had such a difficult time getting past this section that it even touched my scabby sense of compassion, so I offered to trade my one nice large tube for their two small useless tubes. They eagerly accepted, and took off, leaving me behind trying to ride two tubes.

I had a plan. I reasoned that I could lie across the two like a recliner—one for my back, the other for my footstool, and comfortably float down the river. I envisioned myself the envy of the group, each teen begging for the privilege of trading tubes with me. Solomon wrote, "Without a vision the people perish." He should have added, "And with a vision they nearly do." My vision needed prescription lenses. I gently eased down, shoulders on one, rear on another. In response the rebellious tubes very quickly and un-gently flipped me under the water. Head first, upside down, under water, in the shallowest, rockiest part of the whole river. I waited for the credits from my life story to start rolling, because I knew I was dead. Guaranteed, I would crack my head and die, and no one would even realize I wasn't with them until no one showed up to drive the bus. Not only that, but my family would surely be sued by some river ecology group for the damage my head would unfairly do to some poor unsuspecting river rock. I hit nothing, so I stood up and carried my two tubes past this part of the river.

I stuck an arm through each mini-tube, and began swimming, soon catching up with the group. For the rest of the "rapids," all mild, I simply let go of the tubes, floated through without them, and then swam to catch my tubes again. It wasn't ideal, but it beats hitting your head on a rock and making everyone find another bus driver.

Sweetie rode her tube near the front of the group, I stayed near the back. We probably spread out over a half mile or so, but at one point I came out of a section of faster water and saw Sweetie waving at me from up ahead. I thought it was sweet, even though I couldn't make out what she was saying. Naturally, I assumed she was calling out something like "I love you honey! Wish you were up front with me." As it turns out, she was yelling "Help!" It's a natural enough mistake.

A log at that point of the river straddled some rocks at a drop-off, creating a hole between the log and water. Water which rushed furiously through that hole. In a movie, this is where the tube goes over the high waterfall and the heroine is saved by hanging onto the log. In real life, Sweetie's tube shot through the hole and down the one foot waterfall, leaving her stranded on the log, trying not to get sucked through the hole herself. Forgivably, she chose screaming for help over proclaiming her undying love for me. Luckily, Jose, a lot closer to her and more on the ball than I, got her back to her tube. For whatever reason she wasn't thrilled with my performance.

The kids found the river trip fun, but otherwise uneventful. The activity turned out to be popular, and we continued the tradition. We scaled things down a little after that, going with no more than four or five at a time.

Often parents are frightened by the danger of tubing on the river. We haven't lost anyone yet, but it's like giving a speech at school—no one wants to be first. On rare occasions parents have insisted their son or daughter can only go if they will wear a life jacket. Everyone knows a teen would rather die than be humiliated, but parents would rather have their teen be humiliated than die. Such a problem. But if I promise a teen would wear one, I had to enforce it. I couldn't lie to parents if I wanted to keep getting my $800 a month.

At least one injury of some sort happened every time I went. The first time, of course, was the burn. Sweetie & I didn't actually get hurt on that second trip, but we gave it our best shot. Once someone chose to go barefoot and learned not to do it again. The feet didn't hurt when they hit those rocks in the cold water, but later on they warmed up. Stomach and chest scratches from the air valves are not uncommon. On one trip, my son Chip saw a piece of rusty metal under the water and decided to give it a big pull. Naturally it cut his hand. We were about twenty minutes into our two hour trip, and decided we'd just continue. If it got infected and they had to amputate at least he wouldn't grab anything with that hand again.

My favorite injury (yes, I have such things) came to one of those teens properly protected by a life jacket. We learned that a life jacket may protect you from drowning, but it won't protect you from pointy dead trees in the water. The water flowed both shallow and slow in this area, and a bare dead tree, pointing upstream, stuck out from a sandbar. Mr. Sorry-but-I-promised-your-parents-I'd-make-you-wear-that-thing was idly spread out on his tube, when he saw he was floating right towards it, and called out.

He floated at 4 or 5 miles an hour (a guess, I didn't have my handy water speedometer with me), in water about two feet deep. I was too far away to do anything but watch. He could have paddled away from it. He could have stood up. He could have leaned forward and grabbed it with his hand. I probably could have suggested any one of those options, but first I'd have to stop laughing my guts out. At high speed it would have been a frightening event. At slow speed it was just plain funny.

He Twisted his face into truly unique contortions, and did a panicked Tarzan impression. "AaaaaAAAaaAAaaaAAAAA…AAAaaaAAAAaaAaaA!" About the time he had about a foot-long scratch on his leg, he stood up and waded away from the tree. I got off my tube, walked over, and inspected the damage. A long scratch, but that's about all I could say about it. No real damage had been done. The fact that I couldn't stop laughing bothered him more than the cut on his leg. That and the little kids who floated by on their tubes, saying "Mommy, why does that man have to wear a life jacket? Is there something wrong with him.?"

At any rate, his parents were probably glad. He was humiliated, but alive to enjoy the feeling.

Today we do most of our tubing behind boats on the lake. It's more exciting, and I guess it's safer, even though I've lost two pair of glasses that way. Some things stay the same though. Kids still get humiliated and I still get to laugh my guts out. Only now it's as they swim furiously toward that pair of swimshorts bobbing in the water.

The Office

The Office was an interesting place with interesting people where interesting things happened. You know, 'interesting,' as in "That's an interesting haircut Ferd," or "That's an interesting thing you're driving, Ferd. What is it?"

To enter the Office at First Big, you went up some stairs, and turned left. The secretary's desk sat in a large reception area through glass doors. To the left, Pastor Kahuna's office, to the right, my office and another room that housed the copy machine and supplies, and doubled as the treasurer's office. The treasurer was an older woman who didn't act old, if you know what I mean. She and the secretary were good friends, so the treasurer spent much more time at the church than her duties required, which was okay, because she was fun.

The secretary and I had an unusual relationship, for several reasons. For one thing, she wasn't my secretary, but the church secretary. I never understood just what she did or who she answered to. She seemed to be free to define those things for herself. Part of her definition meant she didn't do my typing. That's just as well, because I usually type as I go, and no one can read my scribble any way. There are only two classes I ever did worse at back in St.. Agony Grade School than penmanship: Religion and Recess (honest, I once flunked both). I did better in penmanship because I could usually get a 'D'. By comparison, I got a lofty 'C' in typing.

At the same time she didn't do work for me, she always managed to get me to do work for her. If she needed errands run, I ran them; if she needed something lifted, I lifted it. When the roller on the copy machine got dirty, it was such a nuisance to get the serviceman to come clean it, and why bother, when she could get me to do it? Today, I'm not such a sucker, and would make sure I got a quid pro quo (I'm not really sure what that means, but it makes me look intelligent to say things like that. And I'm sure that if I could get a quid pro quo, I'd like it.)

She was always trying to improve me—get me to wear my hair the right way, wear the right clothes, use the right language, and listen to the right music. She said I drank too much coffee, didn't eat well, and only exercised when playing Youth Group games or occasional racquetball. She warned me, "When you get to be my age you'll be pear-shaped."

"God loves me too much," I smugly replied. " He won't let me get that old." Today, I'm her age, and I'm pear-shaped. I drink too much coffee and don't eat well, and the only exercise I get is when I play Youth Group games and occasional racquetball.

For some reason she thought I had a problem with tension, which I found really funny. I'm so Type B I'm almost a C. In fact, some days I could get a U! Still she thought I was always stressed, and one day she decided to prove it. She had a "mood stone." For those of you who weren't alive in those days, this is a stone that is supposed to change color to tell you how tense you are. It works by reacting to your body heat.

One day she called through my office door, "I'm going to prove to you how tense you are."

I recognized the stone and casually leaned back, holding my coffee cup in both hands, and said "Oh yeah, how?"

She explained what she had and how it indicated tension and what the colors meant. The whole time I'm held my hot coffee cup in both hands. Finally she handed me the stone so it could prove me tense. It immediately turned the most relaxed color she'd ever seen. Knowing it had to be a fluke, she tried for a couple of weeks to get that stone to prove her right, never quite realizing what it does to your hand to hold a hot coffee cup. Finally I told her my secret, and she reluctantly agreed I wasn't tense. Instead, I was hopeless.

Things happened in the office that they never told me were part of my job description. My title was "Youth Director," right? So how did all these other people fit into my schedule?

Since First Big was on a busy intersection in the heart of downtown, a lot of people stopped by for help for all kinds of reasons. I thought since I was Youth Director, the Senior Pastor, who dealt with adults, should handle these people, but somehow, he seemed to always be gone, or in a meeting, or doing something Important, so I got the privilege.

The policy we always tried to follow was to never hand out cash. If someone was hungry, we took them to the burger place across the street. If someone needed gas, we took them to the gas station kitty-corner from the church. Never give cash.

I remember the day I met M. T. Pocketts. He needed gas for his car. "Let me grab my jacket, Mr. Pocketts, and we'll go get some."

"That's too much trouble. My car is on the side of the road. Just give me the cash, and I'll take care of it."

"I can't do that, but I don't mind taking you there. It'll be quicker."

"No, no. That's not necessary."

When you feel like you're fencing with the guy asking for help, something isn't right. He gave in, and we got in my car to take him for gas. I ended up giving him a ride home, because he didn't own a car. I actually found a friend in M.T., and he would come around to visit every so often.

Once I had a man outside the door and a woman inside the door, and they needed to be kept apart. They train police that domestic disputes are the most dangerous, and to never get between a couple, yet there I was. Then a third man walked up. He started so say something, but I didn't have any time. I handed him $5.00 and a tract and sent him off. Scratching his head, he pocketed the five and shuffled away. He probably just wanted to use the bathroom.

Many churches use the "No Cash" policy, and people who like to take advantage of churches get pretty ingenious. One of my favorite experiences was the guy who wanted new boots.

This guy showed up and started telling me a story of woe about this pair of boots he has. I'm looking at them and they look like nice new boots to me. But he explained they're going to ruin his feet and he just needed better boots, and with $20 he can return these and get the ones he needed. You may think me hard and callused for this, but not only did I not care about his feet at this point, but I kind of enjoyed the contortions he went through to convince me to give him $20.00. In my entire life no one ever got $20.00 from me—just ask Sweetie, she still tries from time to time.

What he really needed, he said, was some good work boots, not these cheap boots he was wearing. I called his bluff. Near my home was a little shoe repair shop that usually had odds and ends of good footwear for sale, cheap. We drove there, and what do you know, there's a good pair of workboots for $20.00! I told him I'd front him the money for these boots and he could pay me back when he returned the others. He hemmed and hawed. These boots were also my size, and I began to want them myself, so finally I asked the guy behind the counter if he'd hold them for me for $10. Suddenly my new friend decided that yes, he wanted them after all.

Outside the shop, he told me not to watch. He intended to do something to the boots he'd been wearing so he could say they were damaged when he bought them. "Since you're a religious guy you shouldn't be part of this."

For the first time that morning, he was right. I didn't want to be part of this, and didn't want to be nice any more, either. Speaking slowly, I convinced him that this religious guy was going to damage him if he damaged those boots. We returned them and they refunded him the $35.00 they originally cost, meaning he came out $15.00 ahead! He paid me back, and was so elated at his good fortune that he treated me to McDonalds with his left over wealth.

The pros liked to show up between Sunday School and church, needing help quickly. You're in a hurry, can't check it out, and you've got to help, right? Wrong. If he would sit through church, I would talk to him afterward. If he left angry, and he always did, I didn't feel guilty. Once a man showed up this way, only between church and a pot-luck, needing gas money. He caught me on a bad day, which was a good day for him. I even had to borrow the $10.00 I gave him for gas. About two weeks later, I got a letter in the mail from a ministry in Montana, "Thank you for the $10, it was a real blessing." Yes, it was. When you've become convinced everyone is trying to take advantage of you, it's a blessing to find out you've really helped someone.

About the only thing worse than trying to get money from a guy like me is trying to get sound counseling. Yet sometimes I found myself doing that, too. One elderly man called the church about once a month, and asked "If God is a spirit, how come Moses saw His hindermost parts?" Why should I know? I was the youth director! How come he never called when Pastor K was around? The first few times, I talked patiently with him, but it became clear he wasn't asking an honest question, he was looking for a reason not to believe in God. The next time he called I told him he wasn't asking an honest question, and he needed to stop hiding from God. I don't know if it helped him, but he stopped calling me. He even started coming to church, although he never talked to me. I was only the youth director.

One day a pretty young lady with two (of her four) children stopped by the office. The state required her to receive counseling, and since she didn't like the state counselors and couldn't afford to hire a private one, would I counsel her? Well, I suppose, but she might just get what she paid for. I never found out for sure what the issue was that required her to have counseling, but one thing quickly became clear—she liked men. In fact, I think her main criteria in picking me was that I was a man. Everything else was negotiable.

Fortunately my door had a window, and the secretary had a clear view of my desk, so we just counseled. I talked to her about Jesus and her need for a Savior.

"Oh yes, I'm a Christian. That's why I came here."

I told her about the woman caught in the act of adultery.

She said "Oh yes, that's my favorite story! And Jesus said 'Neither do I condemn you.'"

I told her He also said "Go and sin no more," but she didn't seem to understand that part. She told me more than once that anything that makes something as beautiful as a baby couldn't be wrong.

I don't remember if we ever had another session, but she lived on the bus route, and Sweetie and I kind of took her and her kids under our wings for a while. Her kids rode to church with us, and sometimes she did, too. Sweetie was even there for the delivery of Number Five. She moved and we lost touch with her sometime after that. I don't know if we ever really did her any good, but you can always hope.

One scary thought—not all of the interesting people to visit the office were visitors. Some belonged there! But that's getting a little close to home, So I think I'll stop here....

Thieves!

During my years at First Big, the place got broken into about once a year. Some of the incidents have blurred in my memory, and some have probably blended, but at least one thought has been made clear: People who break into churches are weird.

Maybe not all are. For instance, the guys who broke in and stole the sound system on the day the Opera Guy Came—they were normal. I guess. I don't know, they were never caught, so I don't know much about them. But they broke in and took the only easily stealable item of any value. In my book, that makes them normal. Bad, but normal. Every other time we were broken into, the breaker inners were weird. I don't know what they thought they were breaking in for, but whatever they got, I don't think it's what they came for.

Most thieves chose a popular break-in window off the alley, between First Big and the business next door. Apparently they installed this window just to beckon Burglars. Once upon a time it had probably been a nice window looking out on a shady lawn, or some other picturesque thing you'd like to see from a nursery window, but at this time it was just a nice window that looked at a brick wall about 4 feet away. You and I would never notice this window from the outside. I regularly drove the bus down the alley to drop kids off and pick them up, and I didn't notice that window. I guess that just shows what you can miss when you don't scrounge downtown alleys.

Someone slipped and forgot to post the sign that said "Break In Here," but that didn't seem to be an obstacle. Really good places don't need advertising, people just find them.

One time, we wouldn't have known anyone had broken in, except for the broken glass. I wonder if we had set the window so it would just slide up, would it be called "Sliding in" instead of "breaking in," and would the charges be the same? I've never seen a TV cop show where someone was arrested for "Sliding and Entering." A sliding window would have been cheaper for us, at any rate. Anyway, there was a broken window in the Nursery, but nothing else had been broken, damaged, or taken. As near as we could figure, the burglar didn't know what he was breaking into, and when he realized it was a church, he had a change of heart. More likely, he just realized there was nothing worth taking.

Another time, our first inkling of a break-in was an apple core left on a stair rail near the office. This guy must have been truly hungry. I guess the solution may be that he was a they, but I prefer to think of him as a him. We walked around the church—it's a big building—and kept coming across more apple cores. Upstairs classrooms, Sanctuary, basement. He must have had fun exploring, because he seemed to have found his way through the whole building. Maybe he used them to mark his trail and keep track of where he'd been, afraid of wandering in circles.

We couldn't remember anyone leaving apples in the kitchen, but we found an empty apple bag that someone had apparently left. More serious, there had been a couple of frozen pizzas down there for some upcoming youth function, and now there was only half of one cooked pizza left. This wasn't funny any more!

I can't help but wonder about this guy. He came in the Nursery window, of course. Then he found the kitchen, fixed some pizza, then wandered the church, eating apples and leaving cores everywhere he went. he didn't take anything else. How do you describe someone like this? If I ever decide to get a degree in Psychology, maybe I'll do a paper on guys like this. I already have a theory: They're weird.

We had other thieves once, who were more than weird, they were spooky. Actually, we were divided on the issue. I thought they were just more weird thieves. The secretary thought they were spooky. She tried to get me spooked too, but they never got beyond weird in my book. I'm not sure how they got in—I don't think they came through the window—but we know exactly what they took—two Bibles.

The first was the Old Big Bible. I don't know how many churches do this now, but it used to be that every church had an Old Big Bible up front. These Bibles had to be old, big, and open to somewhere in the middle, probably Isaiah or Psalms, with a big silk ribbon running artistically down the page. The odd thing about these Bible is that no matter how old they are, they're virtually new. From that first day off the press in 1886, they've never been used for anything but to look nice in front of the church, with that ribbon in exactly the same spot.

I also know something else about these Bibles that many people don't seem to realize. They have no cash value. A lady once asked me to sell one for her, thinking that I, as a holy man, would know someone eager to pay lots of money for someone else's Old Big Bible. I tried a couple of old book stores and antique dealers, and they didn't even want me to give it to them. It seems everyone has an

Old Big Bible to sell, but no one wants to buy them. The only time they have any value is if there's good family tree info in them, and even then you have to find the right family for the tree. A church Old Big Bible, being a virtually new Old Big Bible, doesn't have any of that.

I think they stole it to sell, and probably ended up giving it to Goodwill. Maybe it was the same one that lady had me try to sell, and she was the thief! I don't know. No one ever really pays attention to an Old Big Bible, they're just important to have.

The other Bible belonged to the secretary. This really weirded her out. They broke the office door to get in, but only took her Bible. Convinced they were Satanists, she thought they were going to use it in some evil ritual and gain power over her or something. She tried to make me worry about it, but I just couldn't get into it.

"Ferd, those thieves are Satanists, and they're going to use my Bible in some evil ritual to gain power over me!"

"Relax, secretary. They're not Satanists, just weird thieves. Even if they were Satanists, what can they do to you that God can't stop?"

"Ferd, you just don't care because it's not your Bible they took so they won't gain power over you!"

I began to wonder, because if they'd planned to take her Bible so she could drive me nuts, it might just work.

I told her that "Greater is He that is in you than he that is in the world." What can a Satanist do with a Bible to hurt a Christian? I once knew some kids who were checking out Satanism and witchcraft. They wore black and looked spooky, and even toyed with rituals and spells. It worked enough to make me feel weird when I saw them, and I tried to avoid them. Then one day when I saw them, I realized that greater is He that is in me than he that is in the world, and I said a prayer: "Lord, make me comfortable, and them feel weird." I started walking toward them, they looked nervous, and took off. What do you know? God is great!

The secretary was convinced, though, that something terrible was going to happen because of this Bible. Her son's picture had been on her desk, too, so naturally she feared for him, as well. For two months she kept reminding me of her fears. For two months I told her to pray instead of worry, and for two months nothing happened. The issue finally died a natural death. She kept a policy from then on, to take her Bible home every night, which was probably a good policy. She'd be much better off if Satanists broke in and stole her Bible there.

Back to the thieves. I think they took it out of frustration. I don't know what someone thinks might have value in a church office, but there's not much. They could have turned left and gone into Pastor Kahuna's office, and stolen a commentary set or some Greek tools. They could have turned right and gone into mine, and taken some books on games or lessons. None of these items have large cash value in pawn shops. Most pastors are not all that eager to add hot material to their libraries.

Had they turned to the room the treasurer used, they would find a copy machine, paper, and what do you know: a safe! But what does the average unskilled burglar do with a safe in a church? If he was skilled enough to crack a safe, he'd rob a place that had more than petty cash. He wasn't strong enough to carry it or smart enough to open it, so all he could do was look at it and get angry. So he looked at the secretary's desk. There's a 75 pound typewriter with no resale value (this was before your average church had a computer), and a nice leather bound Bible. I don't think he took it to sell, read, give away, or even to cast Satanic spells. I think it was frustration. "Oh yeah, well then I'll take your Bible. Next time leave something worth taking." I don't know what his problem was, but there were probably some apples he could steal down in the kitchen.

There's only one other break-in experience that comes to mind with any clarity, and we actually caught the guy! And when I say "we," I mean We: Sweetie and I! This happened in the winter, not too long after the sound system had been taken. On a Saturday evening, with our three children, we came down to set up for an event the next day. As we pulled up, we saw lights on in the sanctuary. As we tried to figure out how that could have happened, a figure ran by the stained windows at the balcony level. These weren't beautiful story-telling stained glass, but ugly yellow stained glass. They were clear enough that we could tell a human being had just ran by, and opaque enough that we couldn't tell anything else.

My first thought—There's a logical explanation. I know, it's the youth group, playing some game! Wait, Ferd doesn't let them play in the sanctuary. Oh, I'm Ferd. My second thought—There is no good reason for someone to be running in the balcony on a Saturday night, and the balcony is where the sound system is kept. We're being broken into right now!

"Calm down," I told Sweetie, as she frantically tried to pry my fingers out of her arm. She didn't understand I was just trying to protect her, and besides, the bruises were gone in a couple of weeks. Sweetie can overreact sometimes.

It is immensely clear to me now that I should have gotten Sweetie and the kids out of there, gone to a phone, and called the police. Saying it is immensely clear now is another way of saying it's not what I did then. All I thought of was keeping that new sound system from being stolen. I made Sweetie and the kids wait in the car. Car jackings hadn't been heard of yet, and even if they had, this car was safe as no thief with any pride would ever be seen around a car like this, and it wouldn't have outrun an old lady with a walker. They were safe, and could get help if I didn't come out soon.

I slammed the door open and stomped in. I didn't plan to catch anyone, or even try, but I figured I could scare them off. I banged about, turned on even more lights, and talked loudly. "Hey, Jose, you left these lights on." "No I didn't man, it must have been Lawrence." "Not me! Maybe it was Duke." "Hey! There's someone here!" I've never been real good at faking voices, but I was pretty successful this time. I was so good I almost gave Pastor Kahuna a heart attack.

An avid jogger, he didn't want to slip and hurt himself. on the slick streets. He'd figured out how many laps on the balcony equaled a mile, and was doing three miles up there. A plausible story, but I kept an eye on him from then on—one never knows when a senior pastor might decide to supplement his salary selling hot sound systems.

Bible Learning Activities

Bible Learning Activities (hereafter abbreviated BLA, and pronounced 'blah') are creative and insightful things used to drive home the point of a lesson. I've actually done some good ones. The Walkathon, for instance, was a BLA to drive home the message of servanthood. Conveniently we built it around the good deed of raising money for the March of Dimes.

Sometimes a BLA does not do what you intended it to do, and then it becomes a BLAH. BLAH is not an acronym, but a sound people hear. Like me, you've heard it many times; sitting in school on a beautiful day, looking out the window wondering why you aren't doing something else, and the whole time the teacher is in front of class saying "Blah blah blah blah blah blah."

"Blah" doesn't sound like blah, any more than what a dog does sounds like "bark." The best audio capture of "Blah" is adult speech on Charlie Brown cartoons. When I first recognized this, I was amazed at the insightfulness of Charles Schultz and his TV animation staff. When adults speak, children hear "blah." Which brings us back to BLA. We use BLA to overcome BLAH.

One error made with BLAs is working too hard at overcoming BLAHs. Then the activity is remembered, not the lesson. At that point the BLA reverts to a BLAH. Hopefully a BLAH!, but a BLAH just the same.

Once I held a Foot Ball with my group. Not a football, but a foot ball. A party built around our feet. We played games and did various activities, all centered around our feet. This was intended to be a BLA, but since for the life of me I can't remember any scriptural application from this, it was more than likely a BLAH. It doesn't even get an exclamation point, because I can't remember any of the games or activities either.

Sometimes the only way to know if what you're doing is a BLA or a BLAH is to watch for results. For instance, I like to think the footwashing was a very good BLA, but if the lesson didn't get driven home, then it was only an elaborate BLAH. It's very frustrating to work hard at a BLA and end up with a BLAH, but that's the chance you take.

Never use a BLA to try to make yourself look good. In this case, at least part of the BLA is designed to flatter your own abilities, talents, or intelligence. It goes something like this, "Lets see how many Bible words you can make out of the letters in the words 'Smugly Sanctimonious.' What? Is that all you have? I came up with way more than that!" A good word I find in that is "ugly." Since it is virtually impossible to do a good job of teaching a Bible truth while trying to impress people, this becomes a specialized type of BLAH. You simply insert your initial before 'LA,' because it's become a learning activity about you. In my case, a Ferd Learning Activity, or FLA. And since this type of lesson fails to either teach a Bible truth or to impress anyone, it becomes a Ferd Learning Activity Wasted, or a FLAW.

Another kind of specialized BLA is the MLA, although it's not as much fun to say. This is Memory Learning Activity. These are usually done with younger kids trying to learn memory verses, and the one I'm most partial to works best with boys. You write a verse out word for word on a white board, then take turns erasing a word at a time. Every time you erase a word, the other person has to say the verse word perfect. If he makes a mistake, you get to punch him on the shoulder. Then he erases a word, and you have to say it word perfect. Make sure you say it wrong a couple of times so he gets to hit you back, and he will not only learn the verse, he'll love the MLA. There are lots of other MLAs, but being less violent, they're also less fun.

Most BLAs are used to draw attention to a specific element in a lesson, either to introduce the material, drive home the main point, or to cement the conclusion. Go back to our "Smugly Sanctimonious" example above, and use it to introduce a lesson on self righteousness. After the kids have worked on it a few minutes, ask them to share what deep biblical insights they gained from the experience. When they respond by looking at you like you're personally responsible for putting the fruit in the loops, you continue by saying "That's right. You don't gain deep biblical insights from the smugly sanctimonious. Now let's see what our Bibles have to say about self righteousness…"

All major Sunday School material comes with suggested BLAs for each of the three segments of a lesson, and it's your job to figure which, if any of them, you will use. Like me, few important and well trained youth directors will ever stoop to using someone else's canned BLA. Instead, we develop our own. This is because we know our kids and what will work for them, because we have the skills to do a better job than those professionals who get paid to do nothing else but dream these things up, and because we're arrogant. But that's okay, because if we weren't that way, I'd never be able to say that's how we can come up with FLAWed BLAs, and I like the sound of it. "There were FLAWs in the BLAs, mainly because of MAs (My Arrogance, Silly)."

Of course, I've made the opposite mistake, too, and slavishly tried to include BLAs in every part of the lesson. You end up running from one activity to another, until nothing ever makes sense to anyone, and you can hardly remember how to tie the lesson together yourself. For the kids, it goes something like this. "Let's start by finding how many words we can make from the letters in "Smugly Sanctimonious, Blah blah blah blah. Well, times up for that, now we're going to tape a piece of black paper to this cross for every time we can think of blah blah blah blah blah blah. Very good, now let's hurry up and draw a cartoon of someone doing something good but without blah blah blah."

After class you hear one of the guys saying something to a friend who missed class, but showed up in time for church: "Yeah, class was about Some Ugly Saint Monteus or something who did good stuff. Ferd waved his Bible around a lot and said it was all in there, but we didn't have time to look it up."

Your really good BLAs, you want to save and repeat, but be careful not to overuse them. If the kids see the same BLAs too often, even your best BLAs can become blah. I have a favorite that's good enough to recycle a couple of times a year.

Say you're doing a lesson on "The Love of Money." You come up with five questions that each require a different type of answer. Examples are: 1) How old were you when you knew one dollar was better than five pennies? 2) Are rich people happier than poor people? 3) How much money does the president of the United States make? 4) What book of the Bible says "The love of money is the root of all evil"? and 5) If you had enough money, would you buy a really nice car and a so-so house, or a really nice house and a so-so car? These are all short answer, all answered differently, and all relate in some way to the lesson at hand.

Each group member is given five one inch strips of paper, and answers one question on each strip. He doesn't put his name on them, doesn't number them, and doesn't write out the question. (It's fun to watch new Junior Highers struggle with not doing these things.) Once they're done, mix the answers up in a basket or salad bowl, pull a few out, and read them without explanation. Then you jump into your lesson. At every natural break, you pull out a few more to read, and then move on to the next part of your lesson.

I've even done this with adults, and it never fails to keep a class's attention, but I'm not quite sure if it's a BLA or a BLAH. Everyone enjoys it, but I can't verify that it really adds to a mastery of the subject. If for laughs you'd like to see your class mutiny, try this BLA, but don't read all the answers. Believe me, everyone wants to hear every last response. I usually don't read them all, but I tell people they can read them for themselves later.

Another technique is to make your BLA the theme of your event. The footwashing and the Foot Ball are examples of this. Another good way to make this work is to model your lesson around a game show. If you have a bicycle wheel handy, it's relatively easy to make a stand and mount it and make a Wheel of Fortune type game. Cards become clickers. A pencil becomes a pointer. Paper on the wheel offers megapoints for trivia, insights, or activities. The dreaded "Lose a Turn" and "Bankrupt" slices must be on the wheel. This naturally contributes to all sorts of applications, like "Sovereignty vs. Chance," "When you do everything right and lose anyway," and "Is this game rigged?"

We played this game one night when three teen visitors had joined the group. They played along, had a great time, and did pretty well. There were a mix of general knowledge and Bible based questions, which didn't bother these visitors at all. Towards the end when there was a short time dedicated for a scriptural application, I heard a little disturbance from the visitor's area. I tried to ignore it, and moved on to close in prayer. A meowing sound started coming from somewhere in the room. If you've never tried to pray while someone in the room was meowing, you may be taking normalcy too much for granted. I said "Amen" and a blur bolted out the door as one of the visitors fled. The others explained he didn't know this was a church, and when he realized, he didn't want to stay. I can't help but wonder what he thought the place was. The friend who invited him seemed to think it explained the whole matter just to say "He's from California (nothing against you Californians, but I'm not making this up)." Don't let my experience deter you from trying this game. I've played other times with no animal imitations at all..

Almost any game show will work for this type of event, because the kids get into it. You just have to be willing to go to the work it takes to set it up. Holidays and seasonal events provide natural thematic BLA ties, and Lock-ins lend themselves to obvious ideas too.

Don't be afraid of being obvious in your BLAs—kids do obvious a lot better than they do subtlety, and you only get frustrated when they don't understand what you're trying to do. There are few things worse than asking the kids if they get it, and having them ask you to repeat a few of your blahs. "Which blahs didn't you get?" "I don't know. It was somewhere between blah and blah blah blah." That's what I call a "failed BLA."

Preaching

Depths of shame, heights of arrogance. Yes, I've been there. With an audience.

The first time I did any public speaking was in the army. They were trying to get me to reenlist, and sent me to an NCO training school. I think the idea was to dangle prospects of promotion in front of my face, but it instead persuaded me I wasn't NCO material.

For one segment of training we were told we would be given an object to talk about for five minutes with just a few seconds preparation. I'm not sure how this was supposed to make you a better sergeant, but I didn't care—I could handle it. I listened to some of the guys who went before me. What a bunch of goofs! These guys clearly couldn't think on their feet. Stuttering, repetition, a lot of "um" and "uh." I saw myself as the star of the show, being awarded the Sergeant Oscar. When my turn came, I was told to talk about an Indian Head Penny.

I pulled a penny out of my pocket and strutted to the front. "Hi, I'm here to talk about an Indian Head Penny. An Indian Head Penny is round, it's made of copper, it's worth a penny…I had one once. Uhuhh, uhuhh, uhuhh" (I really don't know how to spell this, but it's the sound I made). For some reason, I thought this line about "having one" was incredibly funny, and I broke into this strange laughter, and I couldn't stop. The worse I felt, the worse it got. I've never had one of those dreams where you're exposed naked in public—I don't need one, I've been through worse. I've laughed stupidly and uncontrollably in front of an audience of my peers.

Eventually the sergeant running the program realized I couldn't stop laughing stupidly, took me by the hand, and sat me down. I spent the next five minutes trying to stop hyperventilating, hoping I wouldn't throw up.

My first time teaching Sunday School was nearly as bad. Somehow someone pegged Sweetie and I to lead the Young Married's class. As near as I can tell, our only qualifications were that we were young and we were married. We had no training, no material, and no experience, and were supposed to teach Acts. We bought a one volume commentary, and went to class prepared to teach. I looked at the class of 6 in panic. I stalled for as long as I could, but you can only clear your throat for so long without doing permanent damage. Somehow, we survived

Preaching 79

the three years it took for the clock to reach 10:45. It's hard to believe, but when we picked the boys up from the Nursery, they hadn't aged at all!

Years later, there came a period of time at First Big when I became acting Interim Pastor, and I found myself preaching regularly. I even began to feel I was getting pretty good at it. Looking back, I wonder how I survived. I still attended Bible College, led Youth Group, taught Sunday School, drove the bus, and preached morning and evening services. There was also this woman and three little people at my house I was sure I should recognize.

Somewhere along the way, I came up with a tremendous labor saving device: Don't prepare! I speculated that if I opened God's Word and read a little bit, I could expound well enough to impress everyone with my biblical depth. Ever hear the saying, "It's a sin to bore people with God's Word?" I confess I sinned greatly. Among other things, I tried to do a series on the Minor Prophets, and I possessed no biblical depth. I remember finding an inspiring insight at an early point in one message, thinking "This one is really going to fly!" Well, the good insight started the message with a high point, but what do you do from there? It didn't fly, so I guess that means it fell. Freefall. Crash. Any landing you can walk away from is good, but I was limping.

The next Sunday morning I apologized for how bad that Sunday evening message had been. A man met me after the service and said "Never apologize for preaching God's Word." He hadn't been there that night. Those who'd been there didn't say anything—they understood.

Speaking of being there, there was the Christmas Eve service when no one was. It wasn't traditional for First Big to hold a service on either Christmas Eve or Christmas Day, but I thought it was time to start. We announced the service for several weeks, I lined up a pianist and special music, and prepared a joyful Christmas message. Service time came, and I watched the people file in. I had to watch carefully, it was a very small file. Me, Sweetie, and our kids, the pianist, the special music, my aunt and uncle, and one person who'd been walking by. In all fairness there may have been someone else I've since forgotten.

In a daring move, I put aside my notes, and talked about the wise men: very few went out of their way to seek the child. Apparently the number hadn't grown much with time. After the service Sweetie, the kids and I drove to my parents' for gifts and all. The house was packed. I wish there'd been as many people at the service. People are so much more willing to celebrate gifts than the Gift.

During this time of filling the pulpit, I was blessed with a woman whose goal it was to improve my preaching. You know, blessed, as in "Blessed are you when you face various trials…" Trials like—fingernails on a blackboard, Chinese water torture, getting Girl Germs in 4th Grade, or a little old lady telling you after church every single Sunday that you're "Getting closer."

This woman had a son who was the perfect pastor of the perfect church that was, unfortunately, a thousand miles away. If only I could listen to his preaching tapes and learn from him, I wouldn't use such foolish illustrations, I would use better vocabulary, my references would be more impressive. If only I could learn church administration from him, we could run this place the way a church should be run. If only she could commute—but then I guess I'd lose a blessing. She meant well, and loved her son, but he was a thousand miles away, and she was forced to listen to some student preacher who didn't have time to prepare properly. I didn't learn anything from her that improved my preaching, but I did learn something about the Pastor's Heart—and having sympathy for your critics. If I can't measure up to a lonely woman's distant son, that's okay.

I learned another valuable skill from her: the ability to look someone in the eye, smile, and say, "Thank you." It has served me in good stead, because it seems there is someone in every church with the personal assignment from God to keep preachers humble.

Somewhere along the way I took homiletics, the "art and science of preaching." I learned about properly prepared notes and outlines, eye contact, how to emphasize one main point, and so on. I did well in the class, and now, finally, I'd arrived!

About the time I finally took a class to tell me how to preach, First Big got a real Interim Pastor, and I didn't have to preach any more. Even better, they didn't have to listen to me any more. It was like a vacation for me to go back to my normal responsibilities.

There was a problem, though: Pastor Primo was not quite the accomplished public speaker that I was. I'd learned so many things in my class I was sure would be so helpful for him. I was duty bound to help the poor gentleman.

Pastor Primo, by the way, was the real thing. In his 70's, he'd been preaching God's Word effectively since before my mother put a gleam in my father's eye. He could take a passage of Scripture and share it with the whole congregation in such a way that each person knew God had prepared that message just for him. He preached for weeks on Jude, and I just wanted the book to be bigger. He spoke to the younger people, he spoke to the older people. This man could preach and he could teach.

Still, of course, it was my responsibility to help him improve. "Pastor Primo, I've been taking this class on homiletics—that's a preaching class you know—and I'd like to give you some pointers...." I think I probably looked less stupid when

I hyperventilated about the penny, but Pastor Primo listened, smiled, and said "Thank you." I think he had a Pastor's Heart, and sympathy for his critics. If he couldn't measure up to a struggling student's homiletics prof, that's okay. He had the valuable skill of being able to look someone in the eye, smile, and say, "Thank you," because it seems there is someone in every church with the personal assignment from God to keep preachers humble.

He never said a word about it until a month or so later, when I came to my senses and apologized, having begun to recognize how wrong I'd been. He accepted, smiled, and said something like: "I didn't think I was really all that bad." I have come to the realization he is one of the truest blessings God has placed in my life.

One thing I soon learned about preaching is that some interesting people would like to do it. There was one man I'd never met before who showed up on a Sunday morning, introduced himself, and said, "I need to preach today." I told him, "That's funny, I need to preach today, too!" We had an interesting conversation. He explained to me that God called him to preach at this church on this day. I hit on a response I've used more than once: "It's nice that God called you to preach, but since I'm responsible for preaching here, He's got to tell me, too."

A few weeks later, I was driving the bus, and the same guy waved me down. This made me nervous, because we were close to my house. There are some people you don't want to know you very well. I didn't know yet if he was one of them, but I had a feeling. "I really need to preach down there sometime," he said. "You've got to let me."

I explained if he attended there, and we built up a relationship of confidence and trust, I might someday let him, but I couldn't let someone I didn't know preach at church just because he wanted to. He seemed to understand, and I didn't see him again for a while.

Then I met him the third time. He stood outside the little neighborhood grocery store. As I walked up, he said "Want to buy some bud?" For those of you who haven't encountered the darker side of life, that's marijuana. Of it's own volition, in a move that surprised even it's owner, my right hand of fellowship started to introduce itself to him. I caught it about halfway, before any damage was done. I said something threatening, and stormed off. He never bothered me again.

Remember M.T. Pocketts, the guy who needed money for gas, but didn't own a car? He showed up at our Friday evening service one night, and told me "I need to preach tonight." I explained to him all the reasons why he couldn't, but he didn't want to bow to my superior reasoning, so finally I asked him, "What is this message you need to preach?'

"Well, God is love, and we need to love each other, because God is love, and since God is loving to us, we need to be loving to each other, and we need to love each other, because God is love,..." And a few more similar sentences. It's not really a bad theme, but I told him he needed to develop it a little more; and I couldn't let him preach that night.

He sat down on the step and said "I think I need to kill myself." I explained to him that "No, he didn't," but he seemed insistent. If I wouldn't let him preach, he had to kill himself. Wow. I wish more people were that committed to God's will! Time was passing, and I had to get in there, so finally, I told him, "Well, I guess you gotta do what you gotta do." A few minutes later, he filtered in and sat at the back. As it turned out, his need to preach was less terminal than he thought, and survived the evening.

One of the best things that happened to me at First Big came when we started a service for downtown people. If you've never been involved in downtown, you might not know who I'm talking about; but there's a whole class of people who fit this description. They're not technically homeless, though few of us would call what they have a "home." Often they live in tiny apartments rented by the week. Sometimes they live in these apartments when they can afford them, and in a rescue mission when they can't. They aren't what most would call "beautiful people," but they're easy to get to know, and will love you, if you'll just love them back.

Towards the end of my time at First Big, I learned why, even though we were located in the heart of downtown, we almost never had any "downtown people" visit the church—they were turned away. A lady actually stationed herself inside the main door, and watched for them. When she saw one, she'd call her husband, who would tell them they were welcome somewhere else. The church has since closed, and I imagine a line to an eighth church in the third chapter of Revelation: "Because you turned away those who were interested in Me, I will turn away from you, and remove your lampstand." Maybe there should be a new line in Hebrews: "Some have not entertained angels unaware."

During Pastor Primo's time and with his help, we started a Friday Night service especially for the downtown people. A few people who did have a heart for ministry formed a group, and we took flyers to apartments, knocked on doors, and invited people. We imported a piano player from another church, got one of our men to be songleader and guitar player, and I preached.

Not many things at First Big blessed me as much as that Friday night service. We established a group of about 12 regulars, with others stopping in. Some of the church people started coming on Fridays, and they weren't coming out of duty. Everything was better. Why could 12 "downtown people" sing so much better on Friday night than a hundred "Church People" on Sunday morning? I don't think it just seemed like it, I think they really did! And I think it was because they meant it, and were glad to be there. It's a joy to preach to people like that, and I was glad to be there, too. And they never criticized my preaching.

Taking Care of Ferd

Much of this book has not flattered First Big Church on the Corner and the people there. It's been a bittersweet experience writing this. Sometimes my own emotions surprised me, and I tried to take some of the edge off. I have to make something really clear: a lot of good people who really love Jesus Christ attended First Big.

And, they did a good job of taking care of me. Sometimes, that's not a positive statement, as in "Ferd did what? Okay, I'll take care of it." Like after the New Year's Eve party, when we left the place a mess. I wasn't worried about it, because I had a day to clean up. No one would come in on New Year's Day, would they? Maybe I should have checked the calendar.

Most of the time, they took a more positive approach to caring for me. Even when the Ferd Motley crew was brand new to the church, people watched out for us. We were poor even before I took my whopping $800 a month salary, and when the car broke down, I couldn't afford to fix it. I walked the three miles to work every day, and we got by. Every week a dedicated couple picked up the whole family for church, letting us know we could call if we ever needed anything.

When Sweetie and I taught Junior Church, before I became official, the clutch went out in our old Valiant. The $300 it would cost might as well have been the price of a new car—there was just nothing we could do about it. Sweetie and I didn't tell anyone about it, because we didn't want anyone to feel obligated to help. We wanted to trust God to take care of us. We did feel comfortable asking the Junior Church kids to pray for us, though, and they did.

What we didn't know was that one of the church ladies liked to stand behind the door and eavesdrop on the Bible lessons. She heard our request, and she and her husband gave us an anonymous gift of $300. We know who it was, because they passed it through the man who was then treasurer, and he handed us a check, saying "Mr. & Mrs. Grashus gave you this money anonymously, you should tell them thanks."

Every year at Christmas First Big showered us with gifts. The always helpful Lodge family dropped them off, saying "It's not from us, we're just the delivery boys." I figure it was partially true.

When I graduated from Bible College, our friends Steve & Jennifer took the whole family out to celebrate, and we drove right by the church. "Stop!" I yelled. I'd left my bicycle on a landing at church, and wanted to move it out of the way.

"Well, okay," he said. "We'll just circle the block and pick you up when we come by." It was great improv on his part, because he'd been about to give me his excuse for having to stop. I'm sure the surprise was greater because it was my idea.

I raced downstairs, grabbed my bike, and ran with it, since I wanted to catch them first time around the block. Suddenly, the lights came on, and a bunch of people sitting at tables in the decorated basement yelled "Surprise!" Do you know what 'ineffable' means? It's a good Bible student word—God is ineffable, meaning words can't describe Him. It fails, since you're using a word to explain that words can't explain it, but you get the point. Anyway, words fail to describe what I felt that moment. Maybe the best I can say is I was stunned. Flies buzzed in and out of my gaping mouth. What's this thing in my hand? Oh yeah, my bike. What's it doing there? What are these people doing here? How did Sweetie and the kids get down here? Why am I still in mid-stride?

No one has ever been so confident that their surprise party was a success as those people were that day. Two men pried the bike away from me, and a little old lady led me by the hand to a table.

Apparently they were tired of my one jacket I'd bought in high school and my almost matching Goodwill slacks. They gave me a gift certificate that bought two jackets, two shirts, one tie, two pairs of slacks, and a pair of shoes. I've managed to outgrow everything but the tie. I hope I never outgrow the memory.

During our time at First Big, never making much money and not being much of a mechanic, we went through quick succession of cheap cars. We actually made money on one car. Some unlucky out-of-towner in a new Oldsmobile made a left turn into our old Valiant. The insurance Company totaled it out, gave us a check for $450, and then sold it back to us for $35. $75 bought a wrecking yard bumper and fender (who cares about the color), and what was left bought tires and a used drier.

Later, we were given an old Volvo with a rust problem for the trouble of hauling it, and we were a two car family. With it's own unique styling, this green Volvo had gray primer spots all over. I tried to sand the rust off until I realized that by the time I didn't see rust I did see light. The Valiant was a white car with a tan fender and two tan back doors. But both cars ran.

We sometimes drove a little old lady to church. She had serious osteoporosis, and moved slowly, but was always ready when we got there. "I love your cars," she told us, "I can always tell from blocks away when you're coming."

Pastor Primo got tired of seeing us in a different clown rig all the time, and told the people they should take up an offering to buy a better car. A few weeks later we owned a six year old Buick Skylark that ran like a dream, and everything worked. This car was so classy someone stole our hood ornament! And so in style people didn't even know it was us until we got there.

When the time came for us to leave, they threw us another party. Things had changed a lot at First Big. Pastor Primo had moved on, and I filled in as interim pastor again. Then they called a new pastor, and I accepted a call to Little Church Down the Road. I was hardly even there on Sundays that last month. I was at First Big during the week, tying up loose ends and trying to convince the kids not to bail out on church because I was leaving (I'm afraid I was pretty ineffective), but I wasn't there on Sunday mornings. I feared they might resent me, but if they did they sure didn't show it. "Go ahead and preach at "That Church" in the morning, but be here by 6:00 in the evening. We're giving you a going away party."

I don't remember if there was a pot luck at "That Church," or if we went to dinner at someone's house, but Sweetie suddenly realized we were cutting our time a little close. "That's okay," I calmed her, "This highway is never busy." I was confident we left with enough time. Except it's not exactly true that this highway is *never* busy. About twice a year it is so busy they put out traffic cones and have guys in vests with little stop signs running around. So busy that you'd better allow an extra half hour to move a half mile. So busy that if you're cutting it close you'll be late for your own going away party.

And it wasn't just a party, but also a shower. They didn't want us going to a new church with a bunch of old stuff, and they overwhelmed us once again with more gifts than we would have dared to ask for.

With stunned gratitude, the Motley crew drove away from First Big, a nicely dressed young pastor with his family, in a nice car, loaded with gifts. And ready to embark on our next adventure.

It's Not My Fault!

One thing I really liked about my relationship with the youth group kids is it wasn't just a leader/follower or teacher/student relationship; we were really friends. At least some of us. So the relationship didn't just end when we moved away. Especially during those first few months, some of the kids came to visit from time to time. This was very valuable to me, and taught me a couple of things: First, they really liked me, which is a very encouraging thing. Second, it's Not My Fault! All the weird things that happen when the youth group is around—they're just things that happen when the youth group is around. Lightning does strike the same place twice, and some things just happen.

We'd been at the Little Church Down the Road for just a couple of months, when Lawrence, Jeff, and Jose decided to come for a visit. We had dinner, played Risk, and talked into the morning. When time finally came for them to head home, I realized I hadn't even shown them the church. Half-way across town, this meant a ten minute walk in the cool nighttime. We decided not to drive. Driving might have been a better option at two a.m., when bars close.

Two blocks from the church we passed four guys in a yard who apparently felt the effects of what they'd been doing that evening. Not being extraordinarily stupid, we ignored them and minded our own business. Not good enough. One of them in particular was not inclined to be ignored. Suddenly this guy I've never known as anything but the "Tall Skinny Guy" stood in front of me, trying to look ominous.

He wanted trouble, obvious to anyone with eyes to see, which I had. I personally did not want trouble. Thinking quickly (a rarity for me), I stuck out my hand in what I thought was a brilliant move. "Hi, glad to meet you! I'm Ferd Motley, the new pastor of the Little Church Down The Road. Well, it's been great talking, but I've got to get these guys home after they see the church." Leaving him somewhat bewildered, we moved on.

We tried to maintain normal conversation as we walked down the block, carefully staying away from any subject that might be provocative if overheard. We'd have plenty of time to talk about the big dope once we were inside and the doors shut. Suddenly, tall pale and skinny stood in front of me again. We'd made it to the church parking lot.

I don't remember what he said, but even if I did, I couldn't print it. Mad about something, he kept swearing and pushing me. There's something very infuriating about a push in the chest. I kept telling him I was a pastor and couldn't fight him, all the time getting more and more convinced I could. I considered the three guys with him, and the three with me. I pictured a gang fight. I couldn't fight this guy! But I couldn't move him, either. He stayed in front of me, pushing and swearing. I envisioned headlines in the local paper, the front page proclaiming "New Pastor of Little Church Down the Road Arrested for Fighting in Church Parking Lot!" I knew I couldn't fight. But still he stood there, pushing me and swearing at me.

A Bible verse came to mind, 1st Corinthians 10:13 *"There has no temptation taken you except what is common to man, and God is faithful, who will not allow you to be tempted beyond what you are able, but will with the temptation provide a means of escape, that you may be able to bear it"* (Ferd's Translation—result of too many Bible versions). I kept repeating it to myself, looking for that means of escape, but not finding it. I got angrier by the second, and wondered just what my limit of temptation was.

I was afraid, but not of Tall and Skinny. I'm one of five brothers, and grew up fighting. I got in my first school fight in First Grade (I didn't go to Kindergarten), and my last in my Senior year. My closest brother and I fought all the time, and during the summer we'd fight kids we never met before. One time a kid threw a rock at me, and I chased him into the grocery store and tackled him right in the aisle. Another kid picked on my little brother once, and I chased him into his own home and tackled him in the living room right in front of his parents!

Mr. Tall and Skinny didn't understand, I wasn't afraid of him—I was afraid of what he would do to my reputation!

Still, he pushed and swore. Still, I stood and told him I wouldn't fight. In my mind I went to another passage. *"If anyone hits you on the cheek, turn to him your other also."* "Okay," I reasoned, "I'll wait until he hits, me, then I'll kill him. No, wait, that's not right, I have to turn the cheek. I'll let him hit me a second time, then I'll kill him." At no other time in my life have I actually wanted someone to hit me, but I did then. I needed him to give me Biblical permission to teach him the error of his ways.

It never came. All of a sudden two of "his guys" shot past me, each locked an arm under his armpit, and dragged him off backwards. One of them called out, "Just get out of here, man!" I stood stunned for a second, then took his advice.

What happened? Jose told them I was a priest. I guess they didn't know what a pastor was, but everyone knows you don't hit a priest.

Another Youth Group visit came the day before Thanksgiving. It's good to remember that day, because I know the exact day of my last tetanus shot. Several of the kids planned to come over for dinner, munchies and games. Sweetie and I looked forward to it.

Meanwhile, Buster Britches, a contractor who attended Little Church Down the Road, sometimes got my help to do grunt work, the only kind of labor I'm skilled at. He needed help to put up a ceiling beam on a remodel, and said it wouldn't take long. Well, it wouldn't have, that is, if the 2x4 had stayed in place.

We set the beam on a 2x4, and the 2x4 on the jack. "Just be careful," he said, as he started to crank the jack. "If that 2x4 kicks out, it'll be moving pretty fast." I appreciate an experienced contractor who knows what he's talking about.

When the 2x4 kicked out, it moved pretty fast. I jumped and landed on my hand and knees in the middle of the room. *Hand* and knees is correct, by the way. One hand supporting me, the other holding my head.

"Are you okay?" Buster was by my side.

"Yep."

"Then move your hand."

"Nope." It didn't hurt, yet for some reason I didn't want to pull my hand away from my head. Buster stubbornly insisted, and what do you know? My hand was there for a reason after all! It was pretty obvious I needed stitches.

The older couple living there called through the tarp in the doorway "Is everything all right in there?"

"Yeah, everything is fine, but we have to go to the bakery right now." We should have gone to the bakery just to stay honest, but it would have looked funny eating a donut while holding my head like that.

It never did hurt, but it took seven stitches, put a mess of clotted blood on my head, and got me home much later than it should have. Everyone sat around the table waiting, and razzed me as soon as I came in, but I had the coolest excuse they'd ever heard. "It takes a lot of time to get seven stitches in your head."

In case you've never had the opportunity to learn this lesson, getting hit in the head can make you a kind of hero.

"Yeah, we were jacking up this ceiling beam, when the 2x4 slipped and it hit me in the head." Oohs, aahs, "Cool," and "Awesome." Everyone had a look at it, thought it was pretty neat and me pretty tough. I took a couple of aspirin for an emerging headache, and we got down to the serious business of eating and games.

Sometime during the course of the evening, someone said "Hit by a ceiling beam, huh? That's pretty cool!"

"No," I explained, I got hit by the 2x4 that supported the beam." That did it. No more hero.

"Just a 2x4? We thought you got hit by the beam!"

"Oh, I'm sorry. Should I go back and try again? Since a 2x4 is wimpy, maybe you'd like me to use one on your head?" No takers, but it was too late. The mystique vanished. The Mighty Ferd had been felled by a mere 2x4.

Some might say as a contractor, Buster should have known better. Some will say we should have had on hard-hats. But I'm the one who should have known better, and I'm the one who learned a lesson: it's the kids. When the youth group is around, things just happen.

A Never-Ending Story

Sometimes I look back at my time as a Youth Pastor and see "Greatest Failure in the World." Other times I acknowledge I'm not the greatest at anything, and was only an average failure. How do you evaluate something like this? You can't talk to people about it. If you tell someone you were a failure, they immediately tell you you weren't. In fact, one of the best ways to get praise is to speak of your failure!

If you don't believe me, put it to the test. The next time someone criticizes you, agree with them. "I know. I hate that about myself. In fact, I don't think you put that strongly enough." Before you finish speaking, your critic will be telling you you're not that bad! It's kind of like opening the doors to someone with a battering ram. Not only do they not break the front door, but run right out the back. The only time it doesn't work is when you run into an honest person, and we all know how rare that is.

I tried to explain this to Pastor Kahuna once when he was under attack. He had this annoying habit of defending himself when criticized. "Pastor K, instead of telling them why you were right, why don't you tell them why you were wrong?" People have this uncanny need to argue. If you defend yourself, they dig in to prove their criticism right. But if you condemn yourself, those same people will argue just as hard to defend you! Unfortunately, Pastor K defended himself, and his detractors dug in for battle.

I'm in email contact with Cindy, and one day, about a decade after First Big, I told her I felt like a failure because so few of the group, when I see them, can tell me they are going to church, praying, or doing anything to show they care about Christ. Her response? "You weren't a failure, blah blah blah blah, blah blah." So predictable. She had some positive things to say about me, but they didn't help me feel better. It's good to hear, and nice to think I accomplished something good, but Cindy also doesn't go to church, pray, or do much to show she cares about Christ. It's nice she felt I was important, but do I score her a success?

Many of the kids have vanished from contact. In this chapter I'm just going to mention some of those I have seen again. Some appear to be successes, most do not.

Big Bob was a friendly and really likable guy, but he was born to get in trouble. Someone needed to bounce his head off the bus ceiling long before I got hold of him. It didn't take long to consider him my "Most likely to go to jail." Call me prophetic.

When we moved to Little Church Down the Road, we couldn't afford to sell the house in First Big City. Sweetie asked some neighbors what they paid in rent, and offered them our house for $25 a month less. Shrewd business woman, my wife. It paid the mortgage, and gave us good renters.

Five or six years later, the housing market turned around, and big dollar signs danced in my head. A Realtor convinced us that if we put in a little money and work we could increase our value by $10,000. And she was right! After a year of work and about $10,000 of debt, we increased the value by $10,000.

One day while rebuilding our fence in some of the rockiest ground in North America, I was on my hands and knees, using a hammer and bar to beat a hole in the ground. While face to face with the dirt and my arm all the way in a posthole, I heard a car screech to a stop. The driver got out and yelled in my direction. Being from this neighborhood, I knew what to do—I ignored him and kept on working. The voice yelled again, this time I could make out one word. "Ferd!" I grabbed the hammer and looked up. Like I said, I'm from this neighborhood, so I knew what to do.

Good News! Only one guy! He didn't look very threatening, and he even smiled! Something was familiar about him, but I couldn't place it. I started over, trying to make the hammer look coincidental, and he said "Ferd, it's me!" I looked and him, and he looked a lot like Big Bob, only…nicer.

I had good reason to not recognize Bob. For one thing, young people can change a lot in half a decade. More than that, he was clean, and his hair looked nice. As I got closer I noticed something else out of place: he wore a T-shirt that said "Must be born again." We started talking and he showed off his car: a perfectly immaculate older Firebird, exactly the car I'd expect him to have. Bob always had class that way. The engine shined cleaner than most cooking surfaces. The car's interior was likewise perfect. There was only one thing inside that wasn't part of the car—a leather bound Bible with "Big Bob" imprinted on it.

I knew this wasn't a set up. He didn't know I'd be there, and he had no reason to impress me. But I didn't get it. He was the same Bob, but he wasn't the same Bob. Finally I asked the obvious question: "What happened?" He knew exactly what I meant.

"Well, I was in jail (go figure), when some people came by from First Church of the Open Bible and invited me to a Bible study. I didn't want to go, but then I thought, 'This is the kind of thing Ferd would want me to do.' So I went, and got saved."

Can you say "blessed"? I floated on air for days. The funny thing was, he was so clearly Big Bob. While we visited, a kid I recognized as one of his old cohorts—clearly unchanged—shuffled up to us, obviously stoned (it was about 10:00 a.m.). "Hey man, check this out, I scoped a Rolex!" Bob took the watch and looked at it for a nanosecond. "Sorry, but it's not a Rolex..." He went on to explain why it wasn't a Rolex, what to look for in a Rolex, and then told him the value of this watch. Then he handed it back, turned to me, and we continued our conversation.

He was really doing well. He had a little girl from a previous relationship he couldn't go back to, and we rejoiced in the little girl while regretting the mistakes of the past. He also had a new relationship with a nice Christian girl from Open Bible, and life was good.

I consider Bob my best success story. You might respond, "He's not really your success story, he belongs to Open Bible." I'll take it. Even if he only threw in the part about going "because it's what Ferd would want" to make me feel good, I'll take it. In heaven someday I'll say "You shouldn't have lied, but I'm glad you did." If it was designed just to make me feel good, it succeeded.

The 14 year old catcher I made cry is, as I said in another chapter, happily married and living in Idaho with her husband and three kids. Somehow she found us, and sent us a Christmas card one year. We got on the phone and talked for a while, and have kept in contact since then—mostly by Christmas cards. In the area once, I found her address, and stopped by unannounced.

I found her sitting on the front porch, and had no doubt it was her. It took a couple of seconds for her to place me (I was dirty and driving a farm truck), but of course she hadn't been expecting me. We sat on the porch and talked for about an hour. It was like a time warp. We were as comfortable as if we talked every day. Her husband wasn't home, but the kids were, and I got to hold them.

I remember her as a sixth grader in Junior Church, when she was my first ever to respond to the invitation to accept Christ as her Savior. But she didn't go to church anywhere now. We talked about what churches nearby might be good, and whether she could get her husband to go. As of last contact, she's trying a new church.

You never know where you might run into someone. My dad was dying, and I went to see him in the hospital. They have staff to talk to people in situations like this, and mine was Lacey! Lacey is the girl whose knee I smashed on the rock. Maybe that's why she became a nurse. It would be nice to think I'd had some influence. While in Youth Group, I considered her my best. She was intelligent, dedicated, and talented. Then she met The Boy. If you've been in youth work for any amount of time, you've met The Boy before, because his clones are everywhere. He says he's a Christian, but never goes to church, and the girls in youth group always love him, and it's okay because he says he's a Christian. She left Church and joined The Boy.

At the hospital, after discussing what we needed to about dad, we talked about her. She and The Boy had been married about 10 years, and were doing well, about to move to a new house. No, they don't go to church, but were thinking about trying the Unitarian church. I try not to judge a church by its name, but a church that believes everything really believes nothing, and I told her so. She responded, "You always were a Bible-thumper." I've been called a Bible-thumper before, and it's never really bothered me, but this time it did. I've always seen the phrase as a compliment, and she should have, too.

It was time to prove that, even though I'm not a youth pastor any more, I still can say and do stupid things. I chalk it up to the pressure of dad in the other room, but I said "You were one of my best kids 'til you met that guy." Funny she'd be offended that I referred to her marriage that way. Not only did I manage to offend her on the spot, but I also succeeded in making sure she didn't want to keep in touch with me from then on. It's good to know I haven't lost the old touch.

Cameron lived with us for the school year after we moved to Little Church. He sometimes worked for Zeke, a rancher in the church. Cam is not especially big, but he played football, and kept in good shape. Zeke, shorter than me, makes you think of Popeye. I don't know if Zeke was great for Cam, but he was great for us. When Cam decided to grow a (truly scraggly) beard, Zeke pinned him down and plucked a few whiskers. Cam came home and shaved. When Cam wanted to get his ear pierced, I told him, "If you still want to in the morning, I'll say okay, but first I want you to think about what Zeke will do if you show up out there with an earring." The subject never came up again.

Cam is married and living in a secluded area near here, so I see him from time to time. He has two kids, and works in construction. He had asked me if I'd do the wedding, but I'm a real stickler on serious pre-marital counseling, and he was trying to beat a deadline that his wife-to-be couldn't hold off. I don't know where he is spiritually, but he's not going to church anywhere.

In a small town like mine, they print traffic violations in the paper. I enjoy seeing when my friends get caught, so I read this section. Imagine my surprise when I saw Lawrence there! I took a chance, and sent a note to his old address. I told him, "Next time you break the law in my town, stop and say 'hi'!" He called and asked if I'd been in any gang fights lately.

Lawrence's brother Jeff always managed to have a job at some place we'd shop when we were in town. He seemed to be doing okay, but he must have finally gotten a job someplace we don't shop. I haven't seen him for a long time.

Peter showed up at our front door one day! He'd just gotten out of the Navy, and wanted to say hi! We took a picture of him sitting on our couch, all grown up and holding an animal balloon. He showed up again about a year ago, and went to church with us. He's another we had all the way from Junior Church, and it's great to keep in touch. He said he goes to church sometimes.

Jose was one of the three I inherited when I first took over Youth Group, and the only one of the three to stick it out. Joe was always a key member of the group. After moving, I would see him from time to time, because he had a job at one of the larger malls in the city. He disappeared for a while, then was back. He'd been in Florida, tending bar.

He showed up at our door one day and said he was getting married on Friday, could I do the wedding? I would sincerely love to, but there's that counseling thing. He thought she was a Christian, but it wasn't a big deal, since he didn't attend church anywhere, either.

What I've heard about the Dixon sisters is that the oldest had two kids, but never bothered to get married. I remember the night she accepted Christ—tears and all. The second had one child without benefit of marriage. Little Jessie, who had never been old enough for youth group, was a moral and upright girl attending church somewhere. I'm glad for her, but I'm not sure I like what these three stories says about my influence.

Sally Brown is a girl Sweetie and I had taught in 5th & 6th Grade Sunday School, who then disappeared for a while. One summer day while driving the bus for some event or other, I saw her leaving the neighborhood pool. It may look strange to some people when a big old school bus stops in the middle of the street and the driver starts talking to a pretty girl in a swimsuit, but it worked, and she started going to youth group.

Years later, Luis Palau did a crusade in First Big City, and some friends and I went. Sally was our usher! Doing great, she attended a good church, and had an exciting walk with Christ.

Some of these stories are encouraging, some are less so, but like the rest of this book, they're true. I hope to continue hearing them, even when I don't like what they say. Because I care about these kids. Failure or not, I did succeed at making them "My Kids," and permanent in my heart.

0-595-29401-4